Great Americana

The Spanish Colonie

Bartholomew de Las Casas

The Spanish Colonie

by Bartholomew de Las Casas

READEX MICROPRINT

Foreword

Bartolomé de Las Casas, a Dominican friar and later Bishop of Chiapas in Mexico, is known as the "Apostle to the Indians" because of his efforts to induce the royal government of Spain to stop the enslavement and virtual annihilation of the Indians in many areas of the Spanish colonies in the New World during the first half of the sixteenth century. He saw at first hand the cruelties that he described, for he was a member of Diego Velasquez' expedition to Cuba in 1511-12 and for the next thirty-five years was back and forth between the colonies and the mother country. In 1539 he wrote a work of propaganda flaming with indignation at the cruelties visited upon the Indians by the *conquistadores* and gave it the title of *Brevisima relación de la Destruycion de las Indias occidentales*. He dedicated it to Prince Philip, with the hope that he would persuade his father, the Emperor Charles V, to intercede in behalf of the Indians. This work, first printed in 1552, was translated into various European languages and helped to establish the "Black Legend" of Spanish cruelty. In 1583, Thomas Dawson printed for William Broome an English version under the title of *The Spanish Colonie, Or Briefe Chronicle of the*

Acts and gestes of the Spaniards in the West Indies, called the newe World... This volume, brought out at a time of rising fear of the Spaniards, helped to intensify English emotions against the enemy.

The English edition of 1583 contains more than a translation of Las Casas' *Very Brief Account*, for the printer has added a supplement of remedies that Las Casas recommended to the Spanish government, followed by a summary of a great debate between Las Casas and Juan Ginés de Sepúlveda, which took place at Vallodolid in 1550 and 1551. Sepúlveda, a famous classical scholar, basing arguments on Aristotle, declared that the Spaniards had a right to subjugate the savages and make them servants and slaves because they were of a lower order of nature. Las Casas, of course, refuted this doctrine by reasoning from Christian teachings and humanity. Las Casas at one time recommended the introduction of African slaves as a means of saving the Indians from destruction, but he soon repented this suggestion.

The title page of *The Spanish Colonie* announces that the work is "now first translated into english by M.M.S." But the epistle "To the Reader" declares the work is "faithfully translated by Iames Aliggrodo, to serve as a President and warning to the xij. Prouinces of the lowe Countries." This refers to a French translation made by Jacques de Miggrode, from which the English translation was made. The work was translated into Dutch and served as propaganda against the Spaniards, if the beleaguered Netherlanders needed any further warning against Spanish cruelty.

Las Casas' enemies claimed that his work magnified Spanish atrocities out of all reason and exaggerated the numbers of Indians slaughtered and worked to death in the mines and at other hard labor. Be that as it may, Las Casas gave eye-witness accounts of many cruelties and made a convincing case against his countrymen, even if allowance is made for emotional exaggeration. In countries hostile to Spain, as in England and Holland, propagandists eagerly seized upon the *Very Brief Account* and used it effectively to villify Spain.

Recent studies of Las Casas are Lewis Hanke, *Bartolomé de Las Casas: An Interpretation of His Life and Writings* (The Hague, 1951) and *Aristotle and the American Indians* (London, 1959). Useful also is Lewis Hanke and Manuel Giménez Fernández, *Bartolomé de Las Casas, 1474-1566: Bibliografía crítica* (Santiago de Chile, 1954).

The Spanish Colonie

THE
Spanish Colonie,

OR

Briefe Chronicle of the Actes and
gestes of the Spaniardes in the West Indies, called the newe World, for the
space of xl.yeeres: written in the Castilian tongue by the reuerend Bishop Bartholomew de las Casas
or Casaus, A Friar of the order of S. Dominicke.

And nowe first translated into
english, by M. M. S.

¶ Imprinted at London for
William Brome.
1583.

T   D

To the Reader.

Spanish cruelties and tyrannies, perpetrated in the West Indies, commonly termed *The newe found worlde*.

Briefly described in the Castilian language, by the Bishop *Fryer Bartholomew de las Casas* or *Casaus*, a Spaniarde of the order of Saint Dominick, faithfully translated by *Iames Aliggrodo*, to serue as a President and warning ;to the xij, Prouinces of the lowe Countries.

Happie is hee whome other mens harmes doe make to beware.

Ods iudgementes are so profound as mans wisdome, no not the power of Angels is able to enter into their depth. Thou shalt(frendly Reader)in this discourse beholde so many millions of mé put to death, as hardly there haue been so many spaniardes procreated into this worlde since their firste fathers the Gothes inhabited their Countries, either since their second progenitors the *Sarazens* expelled and murdered the most part of the Gothes, as it seemeth that the Spaniardes haue murdered and put to death in the Westerne Indies by all such meanes as barbarousnesse it selfe coulde imagine or forge vpon the anueld of crueltie. They haue destroyed thrise so much lande as chri-

¶2　　　stendome

stendome doth comprehende:.such torments haue they inuented,yea so great and excessiue haue their trecherie been, that the
posteritie shall hardly thinke that euer so barbarous or cruell a
nation haue bin in the worlde,if as you woulde say we had not
with our eyes seene it,and with our hands felt it, I confesse that
I neuer loued that nation generally,by reason of their intollerable pride, notwithstanding I can not but comend & loue sundry
excellent persons that are among the, Howbeit, God is my witnes,hatred procureth me not to write those things,as also the authour of the booke is by nation a Spaniard, and besides writeth
farre more bitterly then my selfe.

But two reasons haue moued me to publishe this preface,
which I do dedicate to all the prouinces of the Lowe countreys:
The one,to the end,awaking theselus out of their sleep,may be-
gin to thinke vpon Gods iudgements: and refraine from their
wickednes and vice.The other,that they may also consider with
what enemie they are to deale, and so to beholde as it were in a
picture or table,what stay they are like to bee at, when through
their rechlesnesse,quarrels,controuersies,and partialities themselues haue opened the way to such an enemie: and what they
may looke for.Most me do ground their opinion vpon the good-
nesse of their cause, concluding, that in as much as God is iust,
he will graunt victorie to the right , and will ouerthrowe the
wicked. This was Iobes friendes disputation, where they concluded that for that Iob was afflicted, vndoubtedly he was wicked: Which reason is drawen out of a certaine rule,which it seemeth that nature hath printed in our hartes, that is, that God
punisheth the euill, and in mercie rewardeth the good deedes.
Thereupon did the inhabitants of Malta report that Gods vengeance would not permit S.Paul to liue, when after he had escaped so dangerous shipwracke,the Viper leaped vpon his hande.
Howebeit notwithstanding this rule be certaine and true , yet
do manie therein diuersely deceiue them selues , concluding
thereby that GOD sendeth no affliction but to the wicked,
as if hee laide not his crosse also vpon the good: As Iob, the
Prophetes, and Martyres: yea, his owne sonne Iesus Christ,
and that for the mortifiyng of the fleshe , and more and more to
quicken man in good liuing : and for his sonne, to the ende in
him to punish our sinne which hee tooke vpon him.Others doe

beleeue that God wil neuer suffer sinne to bee long vnpunished,
notwithstanding ỹ hauing long waited patietly for our repentace,
his clemencie is at length conuerted into iustice. Some againe,
that it is vnpossible for the wicked to gette the vpper hande in
an euill cause, notwithstanding wee dayly see it fall out contrary: vndoubtedly the Turkes victories & conquestes in Christendome haue no foundation, but consist vpon meere tyrannie and
vsurpation, For although Christians sinnes, especially the great a-
buse in Gods seruice, haue bin the causes of our punishment, yet
must we confesse that the christians, what errors soeuer some of
them do in their doctrine maintain, are not neuertheles so farre
deuoid of the truth, as are the Turkes, and yet do we see howe
mightily in few yeres they haue cóquered & encroched vpó chri
stendom. Also before the comming of the Turkes, namely soone
after the time of *Mahamet*, there came such a flock of Sarazins,
that they deuoured first *Egypt*, then all *Affrick*, & rooting out
Christianitie out of the said countries seazed vpon al Spaine: yea
proceeding forward, they camped in *Aquitain* vpon the riuer of
Toyre: insomuch that it was to be doubted ỹ they might soone
haue caught hold vpon France, & so vpon the rest of christédom,
had not God raised vp that mightie Duke of *Brabant*, *Charles
Martel*, who defeating them, driue them beyond the Pirenean
mountaines. But if we list to consider the examples contained
in the holy Bible, whose reasons are more exactly expounded by
the prophets, we do find that in the time of K. *Hezechias*, although the head citie, namely Hierusalem, was not forced, yet
the lesser townes being taken by the enemie, the flatte countrey
spoyled, the K. and the princes of *Iuda* had no more left them
but the bare walles of Hierusalem. Also, albeit God did maruei-
lously strike the armie of *Senacherib*, and that his own children
slew him in his gods temples: yet were not gods people free from
suffering much, and from seeing the enemie enioy the most part
of their law: their cómons did beare that which nowe we know,
& more then we would, that is what an enemy entring by force
of armes into a land is able to do. But Nabuchadnezers victories
were far others, whé he tooke, burned, & sacked eué the head citie, together with ỹ very temple of Hierusalé, & took their K. P.
& hie P, prisoners, & slu. pulled out ỹ eies, & fettered some of thé
forcing the cómons during the siege to eate their own dong &
childré. Who

Who is hee therefore that dare accuse God of wrong, sith such tyrants be called the Axe in the Lordes hands, as the executioners of his iustice? Further wee see, that those that haue the most right are by the wicked robbed, slaine, & murdered, which is neuerthelesse Gods doing. For it is said: Cursed be he that doth the Lordes worke negligently, in which place the holy scriptures do speake of such ministers and instruments of God. In this discourse of *Don Bartholomew de las Casas*, wee do finde a manifest example. For I pray you what right had the Spaniards ouer the Indians: sauing that the Pope had giuen them the said land, and I leaue to your iudgemente what right hee had therein: for it is doubtfull whether his power doe stretch to the distributing of worldly kingdomes. But admit hee had that authority, was there therefore any reason that hee should for crying in the night, *There is a God, a Pope, & a King of Castile who is Lord of these Countries*, murder 12.15. or 20. millions of poore reasonable creatures, created (as our selues) after the image of the liuing God? Heere doe I, as in the beginning I said, see a bottomlesse depth of Gods iudgements. For it is a small matter to say that the wicked doe molest better men then themselues, for the causes aforesaide: but to see a whole nation, yea, infinite nations perish so miserablie, and as it semeth, without any cause, is it that maketh most men to wander, yea euen astonisheth such as do examine these effects by the rule of their owne reasons. Howebeit we haue two examples in the Bible, though not altogether like, yet very neere. It is saide in the ouerthrowe of Sehon: *In those dayes wee tooke all his townes, and destroyed men women and childen in the same, neither left we any thing remaining*. The like sentence is there also of *Og* king of *Basan*, yea, Moses sone after alloweth all that was done, commaundeth *Iosua* to doe as much to all the other kinges in his iourney as was done to those two. If wee seeke the cause of such executions, man will bee as it were at his wits ende and stande mute. Againe, if men should consider the example of king Saule whom God reiected, because he did not wholy discomfit *Amelec*, but saued their king, and reserued the fattest of their cattell for the sacrifices, their vnderstanding woulde giue sentence cleane

contrary

contrarie to gods, What will they fay, was it not a comēndable, yea, a noble minde, for a king to fpare his brother, either for an Ifraelite to fpare the cattell to the ende to facrifice them to the God of Ifrael : yet was Gods fentence pronounced by *Samuel* cleane repugnant thereto , God *loueth obedience better then facrifice* . And not long before God had commaunded both, namely, that the Cananites and Amalekites fhou!de bee rooted out : and therefore hee was to bee obeyed, and for their difobedience the Cananites remained thornes in the eyes of Ifrael, and the king of *Amalec* whome *Samuel* neuerthelefle hewed in peeces, was the fubuerfion of Saule and his royall familie. But here may exprefle reafons be alleadged for fuch iudgements of God, which feeming feuere to man are neuerthelefle, in that they proceeded from God, meere iuftice. Mofes faith, when the Lord thy God hath reiected them before thy face. think not in thine hearte, faying : The Lorde for my righteoufnefle hath caufed mee to enter poffeffion of this lande, feeing hee hath for their wickednefle rooted out thefe nations before thy face. For thou art not through thy righteoufnes and vprightnefle of heart come to inherite their land, but it is for the abhominatiōs of thefe people, whom the Lord thy god hath expelled before thy face.

True it is, that as in a cleeare funnie light we may more eafily difcerne all that is obiect to our fight, euen fo of things conteined in the holy Scriptures commonly the caufes are to bee founde : but for other matters, as the deftruction of diuers nations among the Heathen : and finally for this fo cruell and horrible example, conteined in this booke, there can bee alleadged no particuler reafon, other then that gods iudgemēts are bottūleffe-pits: alfo that fith he hath done it, it is iuftly done. And yet are not the Spaniardes beeing the executors of this vengeance, more excufable then *Pilate* for condēning our fauiour, or *Annas* or *Caiphas* for procuring his death notwithftanding gods counfaile and hand wrought thofe things, For behold gods fentence pronounced againft the wicked, whom he vfeth in chaftening the good, whom by thofe meanes he doth trie, and punifheth the wicked according to their defarts:

Ob

Oh Asshur, the rod of my wrath: and the staffe in their hands
is my indignation. I will sende him to a dissembling nation, & I
wil giue him a charge against the people of my wrath, to take
the spoyle, and to take the pray, & to treade them vnder foote
like the mire in the streete. But he thinketh not so, neither doth
his heart esteeme it so, but he imagineth to destroy and to cut
off not a few nations. For he saith, Are not my princes altogether kings? Is not Calno as Charchemish? Is not Hamath like
Arpad? Is not Samaria as Damascus? Like as my hande hath
found the kingdomes of Idols, seeing their idols were aboue Ierusalem & aboue Samaria : Shall not I, as I haue done to
Samaria and to the Idols thereof, so do to Hierusalē & to the
idols thereof? But when the Lord hath accōplished al his worke
vpō mount Siō & Ierusalē, I wil visit the frute of the proude
hart of the K. of Ashur, & his glorious & proud lookes, because
he said, by the power of my own hand haue I done it, & by my
wisdom, because I am wise. Therfore I haue remoued the bor-
ders of the people, & haue spoiled their treasures, and haue pulled downe the inhabitants like a valiant man. And my hand
hath found as a nest, &c. So that although the wicked for a
time doe triumph, yet doth not God leaue their abhominable
cruelties vnpunished. But Gods iudgements being in the mean
time such, that by the wicked he punisheth those that be wicked: notwithstanding their wickednes be somewhat lesse, as also the good bee chastised by the cruell and bloodthirstie : it is
certaine that wee are not thereby to iudge that our selues shall
haue the victorie ouer our enemies, because our cause is the
better, for we are replenished with vice enough , whereby to
leaue vnto god sufficient matter to punishe vs: And therefore as I saide two thinges mee thought, and yet mee seemeth
in these Countries worthie admiration : One is , that wee
trusting that the defence of our libertie is vnto vs a iuste occasion doe not in the meane time consider that wee commit no
lesse faults, then those which Ezech. cast in the Sodomites teeth,
Beholde the iniquitie of thy sister Sodom was pride, sulnesse of
bread, and the ease of Idlenes: these were in her & in her daugh-

ters

ters: and she relieued not the afflicted and the poore, and as if we had made attonement with death, we feare not gods iudgemēts. If we looke vpon the first table most of vs may see a great abuse in gods seruice: but so far are we from indeuoring to correct it, that contrariwise some would that the remembrance of God, at the least for this time, might be buried in obliuion : therein resembling the sicke person that would neuer heare of the Phisition, or the children which would that during their infancie there might grow no twigges in the woods: Others terme thēselues reformed, being neuerthelesse reformed but in mouth only. For the wine and the harpe as the prophet saith, are as common in their bankets as afore time, neither are they sory for the contrition of Ioseph. The other is, that in maner euery man generally hath an eye to his owne priuat affaires, no mā medleth with the common, vnlesse it bee to reproue, but not to help: hatred possesseth many of their heartes, and which is more strange, although there bee many in these Countries that haue heretofore felt the manifest iniuries of the spaniards: yet as if their memory wholy failed them, they be redy to compound with thē as they suppose, to the destruction of their confederates, but in truth to the generall subuersion of the whole countrie. To the end therfore they may at the least as in a table behold the nature of their enimie, his purpose & intent: here ensueth a true history written by one of their owne nation, wherein they may learne not that which is yet fully executed in these low countries, but which (had not god stopped their course) they had long since put in execution: and hereby I hope al good men wil learne to be resolute, and amending their liues will ioyne couragiously, not in wordes only, but in deedes also, to repell so arrogant and intollerable an enemie. But there needeth no other admonitiō then the same which the authour hath set down, and therefore I pray you reade him as diligently as he deserueth, beeing an authour both graue and worthy immortal commendation, in that he durst oppose himselfe to his owne so cruell and barbarous nation : and let vs render thanks to god for sending vs so good maisters to instructe vs in our dueties in this so miserable and wretched time, in hope ehat we not quailing in our office, he will also finally graunt vs happie deliuerance.

The

The Argument of this present
Summarie.

He state of thinges happened in the Indies, euen from the time they were most wonderfully discouered: also since the Spaniards for a while began to enhabite those places, and afterward successiuely vnto these daies, haue in all degrees bin so maruailous & incredible vnto such as haue not seen thê, that they may seeme sufficient to darken and burie in obliuion and silence whatsoeuer els haue passed in all former ages throughout the world, howe great so euer it hath been, amongst which the slaughters and murders of these innocent people, together with the spoiles of townes, prouinces, & kingdomes, which in those parts haue bin perpetrated, as also diuers others no lesse terrible matters are not the least. These things whê do *Bartlemew de las Casaus*, being made of a monke a bishop at his comming to the court, there to enforme our L, & M. the Emperor, as hauing bin an eie witnes of the same, had rehearsed to sundry persons, who as yet were ignorant thereof, & thereby hauing driuen the hearers into a kind of extasie & maze, he was importunately requested briefly to set down in writing some of them, namely of ŷ last, which he did. But afterward seeing sundry persons who deuoyd of remorse and compassion, being through auarice & ambition, degenerate frô all humanitie, and who by their exocrable deedes were grown into a reprobate sence, not being satiffied with such fellonies & mischiefs as they had committed in destroying such a part of ŷ world by all strãge kinds of crueltics, were now again importunate vppon the King, to the ende vnder his authoritie
and

The Argument.

and confent, they might once more returne to committe the
like, or worfe, if worfe might be , he determined to exhibite
the faide Summarie which he had in writing and record
vnto our Lorde the prince, to the ende his highneffe
might finde meanes that they fhoulde be deni,
ed, which he thought beft to put in print,
to the ende, his highneffe might with
more eafe reade the fame. This
therefore was the caufe of
this prefent Summarie,
or briefe informa-
tion.

The

The Prologue of the Bishop Frier
Bartholomewe de las Casas or Casaus, to the moſt high and mightie prince, Our Lord Don Philip Prince of Spaine.

Oſt high and mightie Lorde, as god by his prouidence hath for the guiding and commoditie of mankinde in this world, in Realmes and Prouinces, appointed kings to bee as fathers, and as Homer nameth them ſhepheardes, and ſo conſequently the moſt noble & principall mēbers of cōmon weales; ſo can we not iuſtly doubt by reaſon of the good willes that kings and princes haue to miniſter iuſtice, but that if there be any thinges amiſſe, either any violences or iniuries committed, the only cauſe that they are not redreſſed, is, for ẙ princes haue no notice of the ſame. For certainely if they knew of them, they would imploy all diligence and indeuour in the remedie thereof. Whereof it ſeemeth that mention is made in the holy Scripture in the Prouerbes of Salcmon, where it is ſaid, *Rex qui ſedet in ſolio Iudicii diſſipat omne malum intuitu ſuo.* For it is ſufficiently to be preſuppoſed euen of the kindly and natural vertue of a king, that the only notice that he taketh of any miſchiefe tormenting his kingdome, is ſufficient to procure him, if it bee poſſible, to roote out the ſame as being a thing that hee cannot tollerate euen one only moment of time.

Conſidering therefore with my ſelfe moſt mightie

tie Lord the great mifchiefes, dammages and loſſes,
(the like wherof it is not to be thoght, were ouer cōmitted by mankind) of ſo large and great kingdom s,
or to ſpeake more truely: of this ſo large new world
of the Indies, which God and holy Churche haue
cōmitted & cōmēded vnto the K. of caſtile, to the end
they might gouern, cōuert, & procure their proſperi-
tie as well temporally as ſpiritually. I therefore (I
ſay) being a man of experience, and fiftie yeeres of
age or more, cōſidering theſe euils, as hauing ſeene
them committed, at my being in thoſe countreys:
Alſo that your highnes hauing information of ſome
notable particulatities, might be mooued moſt car-
neſtly to deſire his Maieſtie, not to graunt or permit
to thoſe tyrantes ſuch conqueſtes as they haue found
out, and which they do ſo name, (whereinto if they
might be ſuffered they would returne) ſeeing that of
themſelues, & being made againſt this Indian, peaceable, lowly & milde nation which offendeth none,
they be wicked, tyrannous , and by all lawes either
naturall, humaine or diuine, vtterly condemned, de-
teſted and accurſed : I thought it beſt, leaſt my ſelfe
might become alſo guiltie, by concealing the loſſe
of an infinite number both of ſoules & bodies whiche are ſo cōmitted, to cauſe a few of their dealinges
which of late I had ſelected, frō amōg infinit others,
and that might truely bee reported to bee printed, to
the ende your highnes might with more eaſe peruſe
and reade them ouer . Alſo whereas your highnes
maiſter the Archbiſhop of Toleto, when hee was
biſhop of Catthagena required them at my handes,
and then preſented them to your highnes: peraduen-

ture by reason of such great voiages as your highnes tooke vpon you, both by sea and by land for matters of estate wherein you haue bin busied, it may be you haue not perused, either haue forgotten them, and in the meane time the rash and disordinate desire of those which thinke it nothing to do wrong, to shed such aboundance of mans blood, to make desolate these so large countries of their naturall inhabitants and owners, by slaying infinite persons, either to purloyne such incredible treasures, doe dayly augment, these tyraunts proceeding vnder all counterfet titles and colours in their instante and importunate sute, namely, to haue the said cōquests permitted and graunted vnto them : Which in truth cannot be graunted without transgressing the lawe both of nature and of God, and so consequently not without incurring mortall sinne, worthie most terrible and euerlasting torments : I thought it expedient to doe your highnesse seruice in this briefe Summarie of a most large historie, that might and ought to bee written of such slaughters and spoyles as they haue made and perpetrated. Which I beseeche your highnesse to receiue and reade ouer, with that royall clemencie and courtesie, wherewith you vse to accept and peruse the workes of such your seruants, as no other desire, but faithfully to employ theéselues to the common cōmoditie, and to procure the prosperitie of the royall estate.

This Summarie beeing perused, and the vildenes of the iniquity committed against these poore innocent people, in that they are slaine and hewed in peeces without desart, only through the auarice and

am,

The prologue.

ambition of thofe that pretend to the doing of fuch execrable deedes, being confidered, It may pleafe your highneffe to defire, and effectually to perfuade his Maieftie to denie any whofoeuer fhall demaund or require fo hurtfull and deteftable enterprifes: yea, euen to bury any fuche fuite or petition in the infernall pit of perpetuall filence. thereby fhewing fuche terror & diflike as hereafter no man may be fo bold, as once to name or fpeake thereof. And this (moft mightie Lord) is very expediēt & neceffarie, to the ende God may profper, preferue and make the eftate of the royall crowne of Caftile for euer to florifhe both fpiritually and temporally.

A briefe Narration of the destruction
of the Indes, by the
Spanyardes.

THe Indes were discouered the yeere one thousande, foure hundred, nientie two, and inhabited by the Spanish the yeere next after ensuing: so as it is about fourtie niene yeeres sithens that the Spaniards some of them wēt into those partes. And the first land that they entered to inhabite, was the great and most fertile Isle of Hispaniola, which contayneth sixe hundreth leagues in compasse. There are other great and infinite Iles rounde about and in the confines on all sides: which wee haue seen the most peopled, and the fullest of their owne natiue people, as any other countrey in the worlde may be. The firme lande lying off from this Ilande two hundreth and fiftie leagues, and somewhat ouer at the most, contayneth in length on the seacoast more then tenne thousande leagues: which are alreadie discouered, and dayly be discouered more and more, all ful of people, as an Emmote hill of Emmots. Insomuch, as by that which since, vnto the yere the fourtieth and one hath beene discouered: It seemeth that God hath bestowed in that same countrey, the gulphe or the greatest portion of mankinde.

GOD created all these innumerable multitudes in euery sorte, very simple, without sutteltie, or craft, without malice, very obedient, and very faithfull to their naturall liege Lordes, and to the Spaniardes, whom they serue, very humble, very patient, very desirous of peace making, and peacefull, without brawles and struglings, without quarrelles, without strife, without rancour or hatred, by no meanes desirous of reuengement.

They are also people very gentle, and very tender, and of an easie complexion, and which can sustayne no trauell, and doe die

A   very

very soone of any disease whatsoeuer, in suche sorte as the very children of Princes and Noble men brought vp amongst vs, in all commodities, ease, and delicatenesse, are not more soft then those of that countrey: yea, although they bee the children of labourers. They are also very poore folke, which possesse litle, neither yet do so much as desire to haue much worldly goodes, & therefore neither are they proud, ambitious, nor couetous. Their diet is such (as it seemeth) y of the holy fathers in the desert, hath not been more scarse, nor more streight, nor lesse daintie, nor lesse sumptuous. Their appareling is commonly to goe naked: all saue their shamefast partes alone couered. And when they be clothed, at the most, it is but of a mantell of bombacie of an elle and a halfe, or a two elles of linnen square. Their lodging is vpon a matte, and those which haue the best: sleepe as it were vppon a net fastened at the foure corners, which they call in the language of the Ile of Hispaniola, Hamasas. They haue their vnderstanding very pure and quicke, being teachable and capable of all good learning, verye apt to receiue our holy Catholique faith, and to be instructed in good and vertuous maners, hauing lesse encombrances and disturbances to the atteyning therevnto, then al the folke of the world besids, and are so enflamed, ardent, and importune to knowe and vnderstand the matters of the faith after they haue but begunne once to taste them, as likewise the exercise of the Sacraments of the Church, & the diuine seruice: that in truth, the religious men haue need of a singuler patience to support them. And to make an ende, I haue heard many Spaniardes many times holde this as assured, and that whiche they could not deny, concerning the good nature which they sawe in them. Undoubtedly these folkes shoulde be the happiest in the worlde, if onely they knewe God.

Upon these lambes so meeke, so qualified & endewed of their maker and creator, as hath bin said, entred the Spanish incontinent as they knewe them, as wolues, as lions, & as tigres most cruel of long time famished: and haue not done in those quarters these 40. yeres he past, neither yet doe at this present, ought els saue teare them in peeces, kill them, martyre them, afflict them, torment them, & destroy them by straunge sortes of crueties neuer

uer

uer neither seene,nor reade,nor hearde of the like (of the which some shall bee set downe hereafter)so farre foorth that of aboue three Millions of soules that were in the Ile of Hispaniola, and that we haue seene, there are not nowe two hundreth natiues of the countrey. The Isle of Cuba,the which is in length as farre as frō Vallodolyd vntil Rome,is at this day as it were al wast. S.Johns ile,and that of Iamayca both of them very great, very fertil,and very fayre:are desolate.Likewise the iles of Lucayos, neere to the ile of Hispaniola , and of the north side vnto that of Cuba,in number being aboue threescore Ilandes,together with those which they cal the iles of Geante, one with another,great and litle,whereof the very wurst is fertiler then the kings gardē at Seuill,and the countrey the healthsomest in the world:there were in these same iles more then fiue hundreth thousand soules, and at this day there is not one only creature.For they haue bin all of them slayne,after that they had drawen thē out from thence to labour in their minerals in the ile of Hispaniola, where there were no more left of the inbornes natiues of that iland.A ship ri- ding for the space of three yeeres betwixt all these ilands, to the ende,after the inning of this kinde of vintage,to gleane and cull the remainder of these folke(for there was a good Christian mo- ued with pitie and compassion,to conuert & win vnto Christ such as might be found)there were not found but eleuē persons whi- che I saw:other iles more then thirtie nere to the ile of S.John haue likewise bin dispeopled and marred.All these iles contayn aboue two thousand leagues of lande, and are all dispeopled and laide waste.

As touching the maine firme lande,wee are certaine that our Spaniardes, by their cruelties & cursed doings haue dispeopled & made desolate more then ten realmes greater then all Spaine, comprising also therewith Aragon and Portugall, and twise as much or more land then there is from Seuill to Ierusalem whi- che are aboue a thousand leagues : whiche realmes as yet vnto this present day remaine in a wildernes and vtter desolation,ha- uing bin befor time as well peopled as was possible.

We are able to yeeld a good and certaine accompt,that there is whin ȳ space of ȳ said 40.yeeres,by those said tyrānies & diuilish

A 2   doings

doings of the Spaniards doen to death vniustly and tyrannously more then twelue Millions of soules, men, women, and children. And I verilie do beleeue, and thinke not to mistake therein, that there are dead more then fifteene Millions of soules.

Those whiche haue got them out of Spaine into that countrey, bearing them selues as Christians, haue kept two generall and principall wayes to eradicate and abolishe from off the face of the earth those miserable nations: The one is their vniust, cruell, bloodie and tyrannicall warre. That other maner is, that they haue slayne all those which coulde any kinde of wayes so muche as gaspe, breath, or thinke to set them selues at libertie, or but to withdrawe them selues from the tormentes whiche they endure, as are all the naturall Lordes, and the men of valour and courage. For commonly they suffer not in the warres to liue any, saue children and women: oppressing also afterwardes those very same with the most cruel, dreadful, and hainous thraldome that euer hath been layde vpon men or beastes. Unto these two kindes of tyranie diabolicall, may be reduced and sorted as it were the issues one vnder another to their head, all other their diuerse and infinite maners of dooing which they keept to lay desolate, and roote out those folke without number.

The cause why the Spanishe haue destroyed suche an infinite of soules, hath been onely, that they haue helde it for their last scope and marke to gette golde, and to enriche them selues in a short tyme, and to mount at one leape to very high estates, in no wise agreeable to their persons: or, for to say in a word, the cause hereof hath been their auarice and ambition, whiche hath seased them the exceedingest in the worlde in consideration of those landes so happie and rich, and the people so humble, so patient, and so easie to be subdued. Whom they haue neuer had any respect, or made any more accompt of (I speake the trueth of that whiche I haue seene all the tyme that I was there conuersant) I say not then of beastes (for woulde to GOD that they had entreated and esteemed them but as beastes:) but lesse then of the myre of the streetes, and euen as muche care is it that they haue had of their liues and of their soules. And by this meanes haue died so many Millions without faith and without sacramentes.

At

It is a certaine veritie, and that which also the tyrants them selues knowe right well and confesse, that the Indians through out all the Indes neuer ƒought any diƒpleaſure vnto the Spa niardes : but rather that they reputed them as come from hea uen, vntill ſuche tyme as they, or their neighbours had receiued the firſt, ſundry wronges, being robbed, killed, forced, and tor mented by them.

Of the Ile of hiſpaniola.

IN the Ile Hiſpaniola, which was the firſt (as we haue ſaid where the Spaniardes arriued, beganne the great ſlaughters and ſpoyles of people : the Spaniardes hauing begunne to take their wiues and children of the Indies, for to ſerue their turne and to vſe them ill, and hauing begunne to eate their vic tualles, gotten by their ſweate and trauell : not contenting them ſelues with that which the Indians gaue them of their owne good will, euery one after their habilitie, the which is algates very ſmal, foraſmuch as they are accuſtomed to haue no more ſtore, then they haue ordinarily neede of, and that ſuch as they get with litle trauell : And that which might ſuffice for three houſe holdes, reconing tenne perſons for eche houſholde for a moneths ſpace, one ſpaniarde woulde eate and deſtroy in a day.

Nowe after ſundry other forces, violences, and tormentes, which they wrought againſt them : the Indians beganne to per ceiue, that thoſe were not men diſcended from heauen. Some of them therefore hid their victuals : others hid their wiues and children : ſome others fledde into the mountaynes, to ſeparate them ſelues a farre off from a nation of ſo harde natured and ghaſtly conuerſation. The Spaniardes buffeted them with their fiſtes and baſtonades : preſſing alſo to lay handes vpon the Lordes of the Townes. And theſe caſes ended in ſo great an hazarde and deſperatenes, that a Spaniſhe Captaine durſt ad uenture to rauiſh forcibly the wife of the greateſt king and Lord of this Ile. Since whiche time the Indians began to ſearche meanes to caſt the Spaniardes out of their landes, and ſet them ſelues

selues in armes: but what kind of armes? very feeble and weake
to withstand or resist, and of lesse defence (wherfore all their wars
are no more warres then the playings of children, when as they
play at Jogo di Canne or Reedes.) The Spaniardes with their
Horses, their speares and launces, beganne to commit murders,
and straunge cruelties : they entred into Townes, Borowes,
and Uillages, sparing neyther children, nor old men, neither women with childe, neyther them that lay In, but that they ripped
their bellies, and cut them in pieces, as if they had been opening
of Lambes shut vp in their folde. They layed wagers with such
as with one thrust of a sworde woulde paunche or bowell a man
in the middest, or with one blowe of a sworde woulde most redily and most deliuerly cut off his head, or that woulde best pearce
his entrals at one stroke.   They tooke the little soules by the
heeles, ramping them from the mothers dugges, and crushed
their heades against the cliftes. Others they cast into the riuers
laughing and mocking. and when they tombled into the water,
they sayde, now we shift for thy selfe such a ones corpes. They put
others, together with their mothers and all that they met, to the
edge of the sword. They made certayne Gibbets long and low,
in such sort, that the feete of the hanged on, touched in a maner
the ground, euery one enough for thirteene; in the honour and
worship of our Sauiour and his twelue Apostles (as they vsed
to speake) and setting to fire, burned them all quicke that were
fastened. Unto all others, whom they vsed to take and reserue a-
liue, cutting off their two handes as neere as might bee, and so
letting them hang, they sayd: Get you with these letters, to carry
tydinges to those which are fled by the mountaines. They murdered commonly the Lordes and nobilitie on this fashion: They
made certayne grates of perches layed on pickforkes, and made
a litle fire vnderneath, to the intent, that by litle and litle yelling
and despeiring in these tormentes, they might giue vp the ghost.

One time I sawe foure or fiue of the principall Lordes
roasted and broyled vppon these gradeirons. Also I thinke
that there were two or three of these gredirons, garnished with the lyke furniture ; and for that they cryed out
                                                        piti.

pitiously,which thing troubled the Captayne that hee could not then sleepe: hee commaunded to strangle them. The Sergeant, which was worse then the hangman that burned them (I knowe his name and friendes in Seuill) woulde not haue them strangled, but him selfe putting boulets in their mouthes, to the ende ʒ they should not crie, put to the fire, vntill they were softly rosted after his desire. I haue seene all the aforesayd things and others infinite. And forasmuch, as all the people which coulde flee, hid themselues in the mountaynes, and mounted on the toppes of them, fled from the men so without all manhood, emptie of all pitie, behauing them as sauage beastes, the slaughterers and deadly enemies of mankinde: they taught their houndes, fierce dogs, to teare them in peeces at the first viewe, and in the space that one might say a Credo, assayled and deuoured an Indian as if it had been a swine. These dogges wrought great destructions and slaughters. And forasmuche as sometimes, although seldom, when the indians put to death some Spaniards vpon good right and lawe of due Iustice: they made a Lawe betweene them, that for one Spaniarde, they had to slay an hundreth Indians.

The realmes which were in this Ile of Hispaniola.

There were in this Ile Hispaniola, fiue greate principall realmes, and fiue very mightie Kinges, vnto whome almost all the other Lordes obeyed, whiche were without number. There were also certaine Lordes of other seuerall Prouinces, which did not acknowledge for soueraigne any of these Kinges: One realme was named Magua, which is as much to say, as the kingdome of the playne. This plaine is one of the most famous and most admirable thinges of all that is in the worlde. For it contayneth fourescore leagues of grounde, from the South sea vnto the North sea: hauing in breadth fiue leagues, and eight vnto tenne.

A4
B

It hath in one side and other exceeding high mountaynes. There entreth into it aboue thirtie thousande riuers and lakes, of the which twelue are as great as Ebro, and Duero, and Guadalqueuir. And all the riuers which issue out of a Mountayne which is towardes the West, in number about fiue and twentie thousande, are very rich of golde. In the which mountayne or mountaynes, is contayned the prouince of Cibao, from whence the mines of Cibao take their names, and from whence commeth the same exquisite golde and fine of 24. karrets, which is so renowmed in these partes. The King and Lorde of this realme was called Guarionex, which had vnder him his Uassals and Lieges so great and mightie, that euery one of them was able to set forth threescore thousande men of armes for the seruice of the king Guarionex. Of the which Lordes I haue knowen some certayne. This Guarionex was very obedient and vertuous, naturally desirous of peace, and well affectioned to the deuotion of the kings of Castile, and his people gaue by his commaundement, euery housekeeper a certayne kinde of Dromme full of golde: but afterwardes being not able to fill the Dromme cutte it off by the middest, and gaue the halfe thereof full. For the Indians of that Ile had litle or none industrie or practise to gather, or drawe golde out of the mines. This Caceque presented vnto the king of Castile his seruice, in causing to be manured all the landes from the Isabella, where the Spanish first sited, vnto the Towne of Saint Domingo, which are fiftie leagues large, on condition that hee shoulde exact of them no golde : for he sayd, (and hee sayde the trueth) that his subiectes had not the skill to drawe it out. As for the manuring which he sayde hee woulde procure to bee done: I knowe that hee coulde haue done it very easely, and with great readinesse, and that it woulde haue been worth vnto the king euery yeere more then three Millions of Castillans, besids that it would haue caused, that, at this houre there had bin aboue fiftie Cities greater then Seuille.

The payment that they made to this good king and Lord, so gracious and foredoubred, was to dishonour him in the person of his wife, an euill Christian, a Capoayne vanishing her. This king coulde haue attended the time and opportunitie to a-

uenge

uenge him selfe in leuing some armie: but he aduised to withdrawe him selfe rather, and onely to hide him out of the way, thus
being banished from his realme and state, into a prouince of the
Cignaios, where there was a great Lorde his vassall. After
that the Spaniardes were ware of his absence, and hee coulde
no longer hide himselfe: they make warre against the Lorde
which had giuen him entertaynement, and make great slaughters through the countrey as they goe, till in the ende they found
and tooke him, thrusting him loden with chaines and irons into
a Shippe, to carrie him to Castile: which shippe was lost vppon
the sea, and there were with him drowned many Spaniardes,
and a great quantitie of Golde, amongst the whiche also was
the great wedge of Golde, like vnto a great loafe, weying three
thousande, sixe hundreth Castillans. Thus it pleased
G O D to wreake vengeance of matters so lewde and so enormous.

The other realme was called of Marien, where is at this
day the port at one of the boundes of the playne, towardes the
North: and it is farre greater then the realme of Portugall, &
much fertiler, worthy to be inhabited, hauing great mountaines,
and mynes of golde, and copper very rich. The king was called
Guacanagari, which had vnder him many great Lordes, of the
which I haue knowen and seene sundrie. In this kinges countrey arriued first the olde admirall, when he discouered the Indies, whom at that time that he discouered the Ile, the said Guacanagari receiued so graciously, bountifully, & curteously with
all the Spaniardes who were with him, in giuing him all enter-
tainment and succour, for at the very instant was the shippe lost,
(which the Admirall was carried in) that he coulde not haue bin
better made off in his owne countrey of his owne Father. This
did I vnderstand of the Admyrals owne mouth. This king died,
in flying the slaughters and crueltie of the Spaniardes through
the mountaynes, beeyng destroyed and depriued of his estate.
And all the other Lordes his subiectes died in the tyrannie, and
seruitude that shall be declared hereafter.

The thirde Realme and dominion was Maguana, a countrey also admirable, very healthsome, and very fertile, where the

best sugar of the Ile at this day is made.

The king of this countrey was named Caonabo, who surpassed all ý others in strength and state, in grauitie, & in the ceremonies of his seruice.   The Spaniardes tooke this king with great subtiltie and malice, euen as hee was in his owne house, doubting him of nothing. They conueyed him afterwardes into a shippe to carrie him to Castile: but as there attended them sixe other shippes in the porte all readie to hoyse vp sayle : Beholde howe God by his iust iudgement, woulde declare, that it, with other thinges, was an exceeding great iniquitie and vniust, by sending the same night a tempest, which sunke and drenched that nauie with the Spaniardes that were within. There died also with them the sayde Caonabo, charged with boltes and irons. This Prince had three or foure brothers valient men, and couragious like him selfe, who considering the imprisonment of their Lorde and brother so against all equitie, together with the wasts and slaughters which the Spaniardes made in other realmes, and specially after that they had hearde that the king their brother was dead, they put them selues in armes to encounter the Spaniardes, and to auenge the wrong : who on the other side meeting with them on Horsebacke (a daungerous weapon aboue all that may bee to annoy the Indians with) so they rage in discomitures and massacres, that the one moyetie of this Realme hath beene thereby desolate and dispeopled.

The fourth Realme is the same whiche is named of Xaragua. This Realme was as it were the centre or middle point, or to speake of, as the court of this Isle, the diamonde ouer all the other Realmes in language and polished speech, in policie and good maners, the best composed and ordered. For as much as there were many noble Lordes and Gentlemen, the people also beeing the best made and most bewtifull.   The King had to name Behechio, which had a sister called Anacaona. These two, the brother and sister, had done great seruices to the kings of Castile, and great good turnes to the Spaniardes, deliuiring them from sundrie daungers of death.

After

After the decease of Behechio, Anocaona remayned sole Soueraigne of the Realme. At a time came into this realme the Gouernour of this Ile with threescore Horses, and more then three hundreth footemen (the horsemen alone had beene enough to spoyle and ouerrunne not this Ile alone, but all the firme lande withal:) And to him came beeing called, more then three hundreth Lordes vnder assuraunce, of whome the chiefest, hee fraudulently caused to bee conueyed into a house of thatch, and commaunded to set to fire. Nowe on this wise were these Lordes burned all aliue : all the rest of the Lordes, with other folk infinite, were smitten to death with their speares and swordes.

But the Soueraigne Ladie Anacaona, to doe her honour they hanged. It happened that certaine Spaniardes, eyther of pitie, or of couetousnesse, hauing taken and detayned certayne young striplinges to make them their Pages : because they woulde not haue them slayne, and setting them behinde them on their horse backes : another Spaniarde came behinde, whiche stabbed them through with a speare. If so bee any childe or boy tombled downe to the grounde, another Spaniarde came and cutte off his legges.

Some certayne of these Indians which coulde escape this crueltie so vnnaturall, passed ouer vnto a litle Ile neere vnto the other, within an eyght leagues. The gouernour condemned all those which had passed the water, to beecome slaues : because they had fled from their boutcherie.

The fifth Realme was called Higney, ouer the whiche raigned an auncient Queene named Hignanama, whome the Spaniardes hanged vp. The people were infinite whome I sawe brent aliue, and rent in pieces, and tormented diuersly and straungely, and whome I sawe made slaues, euen so many as they tooke aliue.

And nowe for as muche as there are so manye particularities in these Massacres and destruction of

B 2   those

thole peoples , that they can not conueniently be compriſed in wꝛiting(yea I doe verily beleeue that of a number of thinges to be ſpoken of,there can not be diſciphered of a thouſande partes one:) I wil only in that which cōcerneth the warres aboue mentioned conclude,auerre,and iuſtifie in conſcience, and as befoꝛe God, that of all others,which I ouerpaſſe to ſpeake of, oꝛ ſhall bee able to ſpeake of , the Indians neuer gaue no moꝛe occaſion oꝛ cauſe , then might a conuent of good religious perſons well oꝛdered,why they ſhoulde bee robbed and ſlayne, and why thoſe that eſcaped the death, ſhoulde be retayned in a perpetuall captiuitie and bondage.

I affirme yet moꝛeouer, foꝛ ought that I can beleeue oꝛ coniecture, that, during all the time that all this huge number of theſe Iſlanders haue been murdered and made away vtterly, they neuer committed againſt the Spaniardes any one moꝛtall offence, puniſhable by the law of man. And concerning offences, of the which the puniſhment is reſerued vnto God,as are deſire of reuengement,hatred, and rancour, which theſe people might beare againſt enemies ſo capitall as were the Spaniardes, that very fewe perſons haue been attached with the blemiſhe, and leſſe violent and foꝛcible did I finde them, by the good experience I had of them, then children of tenne oꝛ twelue yeeres of age. And I knowe foꝛ certayne and infallible, that the Indians had euermoꝛe moſt iuſt cauſe of warre againſt the Spaniardes : but the Spaniardes neuer had any iuſt cauſe of warre agaynſt the Indians, but they were all diabolicall and moſt vnrighteous, moꝛe then can bee ſpoken of any tyꝛant that is on the whole earth. And I affirme the ſelfe ſame foꝛ all their other actes and geſtes by them done thꝛoughout all the Indes.

The warres atchieued, and all the men done to death thereby reſerued commonly the young folke, women, and childꝛen. (the which they departed among them, in giuing vnto one thirtie,to another fourtie, and to another an hundꝛeth , oꝛ two hundꝛeth, accoꝛding as euery one had the fauour of the head Tyꝛant, whom they called the Gouernour) they gaue them to the Spaniardes vppon that condition and colour,that they woulde teache them the Catholike faith, they themſelues who tooke vppon
them

them this charge of foules, commonly all idiots, or vtterly ignorant persons, barbarous men, extreemely couetous and vitious.

Nowe the carke and care that these had of them, was to send
the men vnto the mines, to make them drein them out golde,
which is an intollerable trauell: and the women they bestowed
into the countrey to their farmes, to manure and till the ground,
which is a sore trauell, euen for the very men, the ablest and
mightiest. They gaue to eate neither to one nor other, nought
saue grasses and such like thinges of no substance: in suche sorte
as the milke of the brestes of the wiues newe deliuered of their
childbyrth dryed vp: and thus dyed in a small season, all the litle
creatures their young children. Further, by reason of the se-
paration and not cohabiting of the men with their wiues, the generation ceased betweene them. The men died with toyle and
famine in the mineralles: these the women died of the same in
the fieldes. By these meanes were consumed and brought to
their endes so huge a number of the folke of this Islande. By
the like might be abolished and exterpate, all the inhabitantes of
the woylde,

As touching loding, they layde vpon them fourescore or
an hundreth poundes waight, which they shoulde carrie an hundreth or two hundreth leagues: The Spanish also causing them
selues to be carried in lytters vppon men armes, or beddes made
by the Indians, in fashion of nettes. For they serued their
turnes with them to transporte their carriages and bagage as
beastes, wherby they had vpon their backes & shoulders, wailes
and galles as poore galled beasts. Also as touching whippings,
bastonading, buffeting, blowes with the fist, cursing, and a thousande other kindes of torments, which they practised vpon them
during the time that they trauayled, of a trueth, they can not bee
recounted in a long season, nor written in a great deale of paper,
and they shoulde bee euen to affright men withall.

It is to be noted, that the destruction of these iles and lands,
beganne after the decease of the most gracious Queene, dame
Isabell, which was the yeere, a thousande, fiue hundreth, and
foure. For before there were layed waste in this ile, but certayne Prouinces by vniust warre, and that not wholly altoge-

ther

ther , & thele for ý more part, or in a maner al were cōcealed frō the knowledge of ý Q. (vnto whō it may pleale g od to giue his holy glory)forasmuch as she had a great desire, & a zeale admirable,ý thole people might be saued & prosper,as we do know good examples,the ŵ we haue seen ŵ our eies, & felt with our hands.

Further note here,ý in what part of ý Indies ý Spanishe haue come,they haue euermore exercised against ý Indias,these innocēt peoples,ý cruelties aforesaid,& oppressiōs abominable, & inuēted day by day new tormēts,huger & monstrouser,becōming euery day more cruel.wherfore god also gaue thē ouer to fal headlong down with a more extreme downfal into a reprobate sense.

Of the two Iles S.Iohn.and Iamayca.

The Spanish palled ouer to ý Ile of S. Iohn, & to ý of Iamayca(ŵ were like gardens for bees) 1509. setting before thē ý same end which they had in the Ile Hispaniola, & committing the robberies & crimes aforesaid,adioyning therunto many great & notable cruelties,killing,burning,rosting & casting thē to ý dogs: farthermore,afterwards oppressing,& vexing them in their minerals & other trauel,vnto ý rotting out of those pore innocēts ŵ were in these two Iles,by supputatiō 6.C.Q. soules: yea I beleue,ý they were more thē a miliō,although there be not at this day in either Ile, 200.persons, and all perished without faith and without Sacramentes.

Of the Ile of Cuba.

IN the yere 1511.they palled to ý Ile of Cuba,which is(as I haue said)as long as there is distāce frō Uallodelid to Rome, (where were great prouinces,& great multitudes of people) they both begā & concluded ŵ thē after ý facion afore spoken,yea wurse,& far more cruelly.There came to palle in this Ilād,matters worth ý noting:A Caciqne,named Hathuey,which had conueyed himselfe frō ý Ile Hispaniola,to Cuba,ŵ many of his people,to auoid the calamities & practises so vnnatural of ý spanish: when as certain Indians had told him tidings ý the Spaniards were cōming towards Cuba,he assēbled his men,& bespake thē: Nowe you know that the Spaniards are cōming on this side, & ye knowe also by experience,how they haue entreated such, and such,& the people of Hayti(meaning thereby Hispaniola) hither they come to do ý like here. Wot ye why they do it:they answe,

red,no,vnlesse it bee ý they are by nature void of humanitie. He
replied: They do it not onely for ý: but because they haue a god
whom they honor,& do demand very much,& to ý end to haue frō
vs as wel as others to honor him wall,they do their vttermest to
subdue vs. He had thē by him a litle chest ful of gold & Iewels,&
said,Behold here the God of the Spaniards, let vs do to him, if
it so seeme you good, Aretos (which are windlesses & daunces)
thus doing,we shall please him,& he wil command ý Spaniards
ý they shal do vs no harme: They answerd all with a loud voyce:
Wel said sir,wel said. Thus then they daused before it,vntil they
were wery,thē quoth the L. Hathuey,Take we heed how euer ý
world go,if we keep him,to ý end ý he be take away frō vs,in the
end they wil kill vs:wherfore let vs cast him into ý riuer: wher-
vnto they all agreed, and so they cast it into a great riuer there.

This L.& Cacik wēt alwaies fleeing ý spanish,incontinent as
they were arriued at ý ile of Cuba,as he w knew thē but too wel,
& defēded himself,whē as he met thē. In ý end he was takē,& only for because that he fled frō a nation so vniust & cruel, & that he
defended himself frō such as would kil him,& oppresse him euen
vnto ý death, w all his folk, he was burned aliue. Now as he was
fastned to the stake, a religious mā of S. Frācis order,a deuout
persō,spake to him somwhat of God & of our faith,which things
this said L. had neuer heard of, yet might be sufficiēt for the time
which ý butchers gaue him,that if he would beleue those things
which were spokē to him,he should go to heauen,where is glory
& rest euerlasting, ý if he did not beleue, he should go to hel,there
to be tormēted perpetually. The L. after hauing a litle paused to
think of ý matter, demanded of the religious man,whether ý the
spaniards went to heauen: who answered,yea:such of them that
were good. The Cacik answered againe immediatly wout any
further deliberation,that he would not go to heauen,but that hee
would go to hell,to the ende,not to come in the place where such
people should be,and to the end not to see a nation so cruel, Loe
here the praises and honour, which God and our faith haue recei-
ned of the Spaniardes,which haue gone to the Indes.

One tyme the Indians came to meete vs, and to
receiue vs with victualles, and delicate cheere, and with

all

all entertaynment ten leagues of a great city, and beeing come at the place, they presented vs with a great quantitie of fishe, and of bread, and other meate, together with all that they coulde doe for vs to the vttermost.

See incontinent the diuell, whiche put him selfe into the Spaniardes, to put them all to the edge of the swoorde in my pre-feuce, without any cause whatsoeuer, more then three thousande soules, which were set before vs, men, women, and children. I saw there so great cruelties, that neuer any man liuing eyther haue or shall see the like.

Another tyme, but a fewe dayes after the premisses, I sente messengers vnto all the Lordes of the prouince of Hauana, assuring them, that they shoulde not neede to feeare (for they had hearde of my credite) and that without withdrawing themselues, they shoulde come to receiue vs, and that there shoulde bee done vnto them no displeasure: for all the countrey was afraide, by reason of the mischiefes and murderings passed, and this did I by the aduice of the Captayne him selfe. After that wee were come into the Prouince, one and twentie Lordes and Cacikes came to receiue vs, whome the Captayne apprehended inconti-nent, breaking the safe conduite whiche I had made them, and intended the day next following to burne them aliue, saying that it was expedient so to doe, for that otherwise those Lordes one day, woulde doe vs a shrewde turne. I founde mee selfe in a great deale of trouble to saue them from the fire: howbeit in the ende they escaped.

After that the Indians of this Ilande were thus brought into bondage and calamitie, like vnto those of the Ile of Hispa-niola, and that they sawe that they dyed and perished all without remedie: some of them began to flie into the mountaynes, others quite desperate hanged them selues, and there hung together husbandes with their wiues, hanging with them their litle chil-dren. And through the crueltie of one onely Spaniarde, whi-che was a great tyraunt, and one whom I knowe, there hunge them selues more then two hundred Indians: and of this fashion died an infinitie of people.

There was in this Ile an officer of the kinges, to whome
they

they gaue for his share three hundred Indians, of whome at the
ende of three monethes there died by him in the trauayle of the
mynes, two hundred and sixtie : in suche sorte, that there remained nowe but thirtie, which was the tenth part. Afterwardes
they gaue him as many more, and more, and those also he made
hauocke of in like maner, and still as many as they gaue him, so
many hee slewe vntill hee dyed him selfe, and that the diuell carried him away.

In three or foure monethes (mee selfe beeing present) there
died more then sixe thousande children, by reason that they had
plucked away from them their fathers and mothers whiche they
sent into the mines. I behelde also other things frightfull.

Shortly after they resolued to climbe after those whiche
were in the mountaynes, where they wrought also ghastly
slaughters, and thus laide waste all this Ile: which wee behelde
not long after, and it is great pitie to see it so dispeopled and desolate as it is.

Of the firme lande.

IN the yeere one thousand fiue hundred, and fourteene, there
landed in the maine a mischieuous gouernour, a most cruell
tyraunt, which had neyther pitie nor prudencie in him, being
as an instrumēt of the wrath of God, fully resolued to set into
this land a great nūber of Spaniards. And howbeit ꝑ aforetime
certayne other tyrauntes had entred the lande, and had spoyled,
murdered, and cruelly entreated very many folke: yet was it not
but on the sea coast that they spoyled, and robbed, and did the
worst that they could. But this surpassed all the others whiche
came before him, and all those of all the Ilandes, howe cursed
and abhominable soeuer they were in all their doings. He not
onely wasted or dispeopled the sea coast, but sacked also great
realmes and countreys, making hauockes by slaying and murdering of peoples, infinite to bee numbred, and sending them to
hell. He ouerranne and herried most of the places in the land,
from Darien vpwarde, vnto the Realme and Prouince of Ni-

caragua within being, which are moze then fiue hũdzed leagues
of the beſt and moſt fertile grounde in the whole wozlde, where
there were a good number of great Lozdes, with a number of
townes, bozowes, and villages, and ſtoze of gold in moze abundaunce then was to bee founde on the earth vntyll that pzeſent.
Foz albeit that Spaine was as it were repleniſhed with gold, of
the fineſt that came from the Jle Hiſpaniola: the ſame had been
only dzawen out of the entrals of the earth by the Jndians, of ẏ
mines, afozeſaid, wher they died as hath been ſayde.

This gouernour with his men, found out newe ſozts of cruelties and tozmentes, to cauſe them to diſcouer, and giue him golde.
There was a captayne of his, which ſlue in one walke and courſe
which was made by his commaundemene, to robbe and roote out
moze then fourtie thouſand ſoules, putting them to ẏ edge of the
ſwozd, burning thẽ, ⁊ giuing thẽ to ẏ dogs, ⁊ tozmẽting them di-
uerſly: w alſo a religious man of the ozder of S. Francis, who
went w him, beheld w his eies, and had to name frier Francis of
S. Romaine.

The moſt pernicious blindnes, w hath alwaies poſſeſſed thoſe
who haue gouerned the Jndians in ſtead of the care w they ſhold
haue foz the conuerſion ⁊ ſaluation of thoſe people, (w they haue
alwaies neglected, their r..outh w painted fables ſpeaking one
thing, but their heart thinking another) came to ẏ paſſe, as to cõ-
mand ozders to be ſet down vnto ẏ Jndians to receiue the faith, ⁊
render thẽſelues vnto ẏ obediẽce of the K. of Caſtille, oz otherwiſe
to bid thẽ battel w fire ⁊ ſwozde, ⁊ to ſlay thẽ oz make thẽ ſlaues:
As if ẏ ſonne of God which died foz euery one of thẽ had cõman-
ded in his law, wher he ſaith, Go teach al nations, ẏ there ſhou'd
be ozdinãces ſet down vnto infidels, being peacefull ⁊ quiet, ⁊ in
poſſeſſion of their pzoper lande, if ſo be they receiued it not foozth
with, wout any pzeaching oz teaching firſt had: ⁊ if ẏ they ſubmit-
ted not thẽſelues to ẏ dominiõ of a king, whõ they neuer ſawe ⁊
whom they neuer heard ſpeake of, ⁊ namely ſuch a one as whoſe
meſſengers ⁊ mẽ were ſo cruel, ⁊ ſo debarred frõ all pitie, ⁊ ſuch
hozrible tyzãts, ẏ they ſhould foz ẏ loſe their goods ⁊ lands, their
liberty, their wiues ⁊ childzẽ, w their liues. Which is a thing too
abſurd ⁊ fond, wozthy of al repzoch ⁊ mockery, yea wozthy of hel
fire, in ſuch ſoze as whẽ this wicked and wzetched gouernour had

accepted the charge, to put in execution the sayde ordinances, to the end to make them seeme ỹ more iust in appearance. For they were of thēselues impertinent, against all reason ẽ law, he commanded (or peraduenture ỹ thieues, whom he dispatched to doe ỹ executiõ, did it of their own heads) whē they were purposed to go a rouing ẽ robbing of any place, where they knewe ỹ there was any gold, ỹ Indians being in their towns ẽ dwelling houses, without mistrusting any thing, ỹ wicked Spaniards would go after ỹ guise of thieues, vnto within halfe a league neere some town, borowe, or village, and there by themselues alone, ẽ by night make a reading, publication, or proclamation of ỹ said ordinances, saying thus, Oyes Caciques ẽ Indians of this firme land of such a place: Be it knowen vnto you, that there is one God, one Pope, one king of Castile, which is L. of these landes : make your appearance, al delay set aside, here to do him homage, ẽc. Which if you shall not accomplish: Be it knowen vnto you, ỹ we wil make war vpõ you, and we wil kil you, ẽ make you slaues. Hereupon at the fourth watch in ỹ morning, the poore innocents, sleeping yet with their wiues and children : these tyrantes set vppon the place, casting fire on the houses which commonly were thatched, ẽ so burn vp all quick men, womē ẽ children, more sodainely thē that they could of a great many be perceiued. They massacred at the instant those that seemed thē good, ẽ those whõ they took prisonners, they caused thē cruelly to die vpõ ỹ rack, to make thē to tell in what places there were any more golde thē they found wt them: and others which remayned aliue, they made them slaues, marking them with a hot iron, so after the fire being out ẽ quenched, they go seeke the golde in their houses. This is then the deportement in these affayres of this mischieuous person, with all the bond of his vngodly Christians, which hee trayned from the fourteenth yeere, vnto the one and twentie, or two and twentieth yeere, sending in these exploytes fire or moe of his seruants or souldiers, by whom he receiued as many shares, ouer and besides his Capeaynes Generalles part, which he leuied of all the golde, of all the pearles, and of all the iewels which they tooke of those whom they made their slaues. The selfsame did ỹ kings officers, euery one sending forth as many seruants as he coulde.

The

The Byshoppe also, which was the chiefe in the Realme, hee sent his seruauntes to haue his share in the bootie : They spoyled more golde within the tyme, and in this realme, as farre foorth as I am able to recken, then woulde amount to a million of Ducates, yea, I beleeue, that I make my reckoning with the least. Yet will it bee founde, that of all this great thieuing, they neuer sent to the king ought saue three thousande Castillans, hauing there about killed and destroyed aboue eyght hundred thousande soules.

The other tyraunt gouernours which succeeded after, vnto the yeere thirtie and three, slue, or at least wise consented, for all those which remayned to slay them in that tyrannicall slauerie.

Amongst an infinite sorte of mischiefes, which this gouernoure did, or consented vnto the doing during the time of his gouernment, this was one: To witte, that a Cacike or Lorde giuing him, eyther of his good will, or whiche is rather to bee thought for feare, the weight of niene thousande Ducates: the Spaniardes not content withall, tooke the saide Lorde, and tyed him to a stake, setting him on the earth, his feete stretched vp, against the which they set fire to cause him to giue them some more golde. The Lorde sent to his house, whence there were brought yet moreouer three thousand Castillans. They goe a freshe to giue him newe tormentes. And when the Lorde gaue them no more, eyther because he had it not, or because hee woulde giue them no more, they bent his feete agaynst the fyre, vntill that the very marrowe sprang out and trylled downe the sowles of his feete : so as hee therewith died. They haue oftentimes exercised these kinde of tormentes towardes the Lordes, to make them giue them golde, wherewith they haue also slayne them.

An other tyme, a certayne companie of Spaniardes, vsing their theftes and robberies, came to a mountayne, where were assembled and hid a number of people, hauing shunned those men so pernicious and horrible : whom incontinent entring vpon, they tooke a three or fourescore, as well women as mayds, hauing killed as many as they could kill.

The morrowe after, there assembled a great companie of

Indi-

Indians, to pursue the Spaniardes, warring against them for the great desire they had to recouer their wiues and daughters.

The Spaniards perceiuing the Indians to approche so neere vpon them, would not so forgo their pray, but stabd their swords thorowe the bellies of the wiues and wenches, leauing but one alone aliue of all the fourescore. The Indians felt their hearts to burst for sorrowe and griefe which they suffered, yelling out in cries and speaking suche woordes: O wicked men, O yee the cruell Spaniardes: doe yee kill Las Iras: They terme Iras in that countrey the women: as if they woulde say, To kyll women, those be actes of abhominable men, and cruell as beastes.

There was a tenne or fifteene leagues from Joanama, a great Lorde named Paris, which was very riche of golde: The Spaniardes went thither, whome this Lorde receiued as if they had been his own brethren, and made a present vnto the Captaine of fiftie thousand Castillans of his own voluntarie accord. It seemed vnto the Captaine and the other Spaniardes, that he which gaue such a great summe of his owne will, shoulde haue a great treasure, which shoulde be the ende and easing of their traueyles. They make wise, and pretende in wordes to depart: but they returne at the fourth watch of the morning, setting vpon the towne which mistrusted nothing, set it on fire, whereby was burnt and slayne a great number of people, & by this meanes they brought away in the spoyle fiftie, or threescore thousand Castillans moe.

The Cacik or Lorde escaped without being slayne or taken, and leuied incontinent as many of his as he coulde. And at the ende of three or foure dayes, ouertaketh the Spaniardes whiche had taken from him an hundreth and thirtie, or fourtie thousande Castillans, and set vppon them valiantly, killing fiftie Spaniardes, and recouering all the golde whiche they had taken from him. The others saued them selues by running away, beyng well charged with blowes and wounded.

Not long after, diuers of the Spanishe returne against the saide Cacik, and discomfite him with an infinite number of his people. Those which were not slayne, they put them to the ordinarie bondage: in such sort, as that there is not at this day, neyther

ther

ther track nor token, that there hath bin liuing there eyther people, or so much as one man alone borne of woman within thirtie
leagues of the lande, which was before notably peopled and gouerned by diuers Lordes. There is no reconing able to be made
of the murders which this caitiffe with his companie committed
in these realmes which he so dispeopled.

Of the prouince of Nica-
ragua.

The yeere a thousande, fiue hundred, twentie and two, or
twentie three, this tyraunt went farder into the lande : to
bring vnder his yoke the most fertile prouince of Nicaragua, &
so in thither hee entred in an euill houre. There is no man which
is able worthely and sufficiently to speake of the fertiltie, health-
somenesse, prosperitie, and frequencie, of those nations that
there were.

It was a thing wonderfull to beholde, howe well it was peopled, hauing townes of three or foure leagues in length, full of
maruilous fruites, which fruites were also the cause of the frequencie of the people. These people, for as muche as the countrey was flatte and leuell, hauing no hilles where any might
hide them, and for that it was so pleasant and delectable, that the
natiue inhabitauntes coulde not abandon it but with great heart
griefe and difficultie, for which cause they the rather endured and
suffered grieuons persecutions, supporting as muche as they
coulde, the tyrannies and seruitudes, inflicted by the Spanishe
Also for that by their nature they were verye softe natured and
peaceable people, these (I say) this tyraunt with his mates
made to endure (that which hee had vsed also to doe to destroy
likewise other realmes) so many dammages, so many murders,
so many cruelties, so many slaueries and iniquities, that there is
no humane tongue is able to discipher them. He sent fiftie horsemen, and caused to slay all the people of this prouince, (which is
greater then the countye of Rossillon) with the swoorde : in
such sort, as that he left aliue, nor man, nor woman, nor olde, nor
young

young for the least cause in the world: as if they came not incontinent at his commaunde: or if they did not bring him so many load of Mahis, which signifieth in that country bread corne:or if they did not bring him so many Indians to serue him and others of his company: for the countrey lay leuell, as was sayde, and no creature coulde escape his horses and diuelishe rage.

He sent Spaniardes to make out roades, that is to say,to go a thieuing into other prouinces : and gaue leaue to those rouers, to carrie with them as many Indians of this peaceable people as they listed, and that they shoulde serue them, whome they put to the chayne, to the ende they shoulde not giue ouer the burdens of three or fourescore poundes wei ght, wherewith they loded them, whereof it came to passe oftentimes that of foure thousand Indians, there returned not home to their housen sixe on liue:but euen fell downe starke dead in the high way: and when any were so wearie that they coulde march no farther for the lieast of their burdens,or that some of them fell sicke, or fainted for hunger or thyrst, because it should not neede to stande so long as to vnlocke the chaine, and to make the speedier dispatch, hee cut off the head from y shoulders, and so the head tumbled downe one way, and the bodie another. Now consider with your selues, what the other pore soules might thinke the whiles. Certainely whē as he vsed to speede out such voiages, y Indians knowing y none in a maner euer returned home again, at parting one frō another they would weep and sigh, saying: such waies are y same where as we were wont to serue y christians, & howbeit we traueiled sore there: yet that notwithstanding we came home again to our housen, our wiues and our children : but nowe wee goe without hope euer to returne againe to see thē, & to liue together with them.

At a time when he woulde make a newe sharing forth of the Indians, because his pleasure was such, yea men say that it was in deede to ridde the Indians, as those to whome hee meant no good at all, but to giue them away to whome he sawe good : hee was the cause that the Indians sowed not their groundes one whole yeeres continuance.

So as nowe, when they wanted bread, the Spaniards tooke away from the Indians their Mahis, which they had in store for prouision, to nourishe them and their children: whereby there dyed of famine, more then twentie or thirtie thousande soules. And it came to passe, that a woman fallen madde with the famin, slue her sonne to eate him.

Forasmuch as euery towneshippe, and all other places inhabited that the Spaniardes had in their subiection, was none other then a very garden of pleasure (as hath bin sayd) they kept them selues euery one forsooth in the place estheated to him in partition (or as they vse to speake) giuen him in commaund, and did their affayres, nourishing themselues with the goods and prouisions of the poore Indians. In this wise did they take the landes and inheritaunces perticuler wherewith they sustayned themselues, so as the Spaniardes kept in their owne houses, all the Indians, Lords, old men, women, and children, causing them to serue them day and night without rest, euen to the infantes as soone as they coulde but goe, to put them to the greatest thing they were able to doe: yea and to greater thinges then they were able to doe. And thus haue they consumed and abolished, and doe yet euery day vnto this present, consume and abolish the few remayning behind, not permitting thē to retayn house nor ought els that is their owne. Wherein they may vaunt to haue surmounted them selues, in their owne iniquities and vnrighteousnesse by them wrought in Hispaniola.

They haue discomfited and oppressed in this prouince a great number of people, and hastened their death in cawsing them to beare boordes and tymber vnto the hauen thirtie leagues distance, to make shippes with: and sent them to goe seeke honnie and waxe amiddest the mountaines, where the Tigres deuoured them: Yea they haue laden women with childe, and women new deliuered or lying in, with burdens enough for beasts.

The greatest plague whiche hath most dispeopled this prouince, hath beene the licence whcih the gouernour gaue to the Spaniardes, to demaunde or exact of the Cacikes and Lordes of the countrey slaues. They did giue them euery foure or fiue moneths, or as often times as euery one coulde obtayne licence

of

of the gouernour fiftie ſlaues : with thzeatninges, that if they
gaue them not, they woulde burne them aliue, oz cauſe them to
bee eaten with dogges.

Nowe ozdinarily the Indians doe not keepe ſlaues,
and it is muche if one Cacike doe keepe two, thzee, oz foure:
Wherefoze to ſerue this turne, they went to theyz ſubiectes, and
tooke firſt all the Dzphelins, and afterwards they exacted of him
that had two childzen one, and of him that had thzee, two: and in
this maner was the Cacike fayne to furniſhe ſtill to the number
that the tyzane impoſed, with the great weeping and crying of
the people: foz they are people that doe loue (as it ſeemeth) ten-
derly their childzen. And foz becauſe that this was done continually, they diſpeopled from the yeere 23.vnto the yeere 33.
all this realme. Foz there went foz ſixe oz ſeuen yeeres ſpace,
fiue oz ſixe ſhippes at a time, carrying foozth great numbers of
thoſe Indians, foz to ſell them foz ſlaues at Joanama and Peru:
where they all dyed not long after. Foz it is a thing pzooued
and experimented a thouſande times, that when the Indians
are tranſpozted from their naturall countrey, they ſoone ende
their liues: beſides that theſe giue them not their ſuſtenance,
neyther yet diminiſh they of their toyle, as neyther doe they buy
them foz ought elſe but to toyle. They haue by this maner
of doing dzawen out of this pzouince of the Indies, whome they
haue made ſlaues, being as free bozne as I am, moze then fiue
hundzeth thouſande ſoules. And by the diueliſhe warres which
the Spaniſhe haue made on them, and the hidious thzaledome
that they haue laid vpon them, they haue bzought to their deaths,
other fiftie oz thzeeſcoze thouſande perſons, and doe yet dayly
make hauocke of them at this pzeſent. Al theſe ſlaughters haue
been accompliſhed within the ſpace of fourteene yeeres. There
may be left at this day in all this pzouinces of Nicaragua, the
number of a foure oz fiue thouſande perſons, whiche they alſo
cauſe to die as yet euery day, through bondages and oppzeſſions
ozdinarily and perſonall, hauing bin the countrey the moſt peopled in the wozlde, as I haue already ſaide.

D   Of

Of newe Spayne.

IN the yeere one thousande, fiue hundred and seuenteene, was newe Spaine discouered : at the discouerie whereof were committed great disorders and slaughters of the Indians, by those which had the doing of that exploit. The yeere a thousande, fiue hundred, and eyghteene, there went Spanish Christians (as they terme them selues,) to rob and slay, notwithstanding that they sayde they went to people the countrey. Sithence that yere, a thousande, fiue hundred, & eyghteen, vnto this present the yeere a thousande, fiue hundreth, fourtie two, the vniust dealings, the violencie, and the tyrannies which the Spaniardes haue wrought against the Indians, are mounted to the highest degree of extremitie: those selfe same Spaniardes, hauing thorowly lost the feare of God, and of the king, and forgotten themselues. For the discomfitures, cruelties, slaughters, spoyles, the destructions of Cities, pillages, violences, and tyrannies which they haue made in so many realms, and so great, hath bin such & so horrible, that all ÿ things which we haue spoke of, are nothing in comparison of those which haue bin done and executed frõ the yere 1518, vnto the yere 1542. & as yet at this time, this moneth current of September, are in doing & committing ÿ most grieuousest, & the most abominablest of al: in such sort ÿ the rule whiche we set down before is verified: That is, that from the beginning they haue alwaies proceeded frõ euil to worse, & haue gone beyond thẽselues in ÿ most greatest disorders & diuelish doings.

In such wise, as that since the first entring into new Spaine, wi was on the eight day of April, in ÿ 18. yeere, vnto ÿ 13. yeere, which make 12. yeeres complete : the slaughters & the destructions haue neuer ceased, which the bloodie and cruel handes of ÿ Spaniardes haue continually executed in 400, and 50. leagues of land or there about in cõpasse, roũd about Mexico, & the neighbour regions round about, such as the which might contayne 4. or 5. great realmes, as great & a great deale farre fertiler then is Spain. All this countrey was more peopled with inhabitantes,

then

then Toledo, and Seuill, and Ualadolyd, and Sauagoce, with Barcelona . For that there hath not beene commonly in those cities, nor neuer were such a worlde of people, when they haue beene peopled with the most , as there was then in the sayde countrey, which contayneth in the whole compasse more then one thousande eyght hundred leagues : during the time of the aboue mentioned twelue yeeres, the Spaniardes haue slaine & done to death in the sayd hundred & fiftie leagues of land what men, what women, what young and litle children, more then foure millions of soules , with the dint of the sworde and speare, & by fire, during (I say) the conquests (as they call them) but rather in deede during the routes of barbarous tyrantes, suche as are condemned not onely by the law of God, but also by all laws of man, and are worser then those which are done by the Turke to destroy the church of Christ. Neyther yet doe I here comprise those, whom they haue slayne, and do slay as yet euery day, in the aforesaid slauerie and oppression ordinary.

There is no tongue, skill, knowledge, nor industrie of man, which is able to recount the particularities of the dreadfull dooings, which these arrand enemies, yea deadly enemies of mankinde haue put in vre generally throughout and in diuers parts, and at diuers times within the saide compasse of grounde, specially some of the deedes done, because of their circumstances whiche make them become the more haynous, can not be well as it ought to be disciphred by any diligence, leasure, or quoting what soeuer that may be thereto employed. Howebeit I will rehearse some things of certayne parties, but vnder protestation, & as if I were sworne solemnly to tell the trueth, that is, that I doe beleeue that I shal not when I haue all done, touch one only point of a thousande.

Of newe Spaine in particular.

Amongst other murderers & massacres they committed this one which I am now to speak of, in a great citie more then of a thirtie

thou-

thousande householdes, which is called Cholula : that is, that, comming before them the Lordes of the countrey and places nere adioyning, and first and formost the Priestes with their chiefe high priest in procession, to receiue the Spaniardes with great solemnitie and reuerence, so conducting them in the middest of them, towardes their lodgings in the citie, in the housen and place of the Lorde, or other principall Lordes of the Citie : the Spaniardes aduised with themselues to make a massacre, or a chastise (as they speake) to the ende, to raise and plant a dread of their cruelties in euery corner of all that countrey.

Nowe this hath been alwayes their customary maner of doyng, in euery the regions which they haue entred into, to exe-cute incontinent vpon their first arriuall, some notable cruell butcherie, to the ende, that those poore and innocent lambes should tremble for feare whiche they should haue of them: in this wise they sent first to common all the Lordes and Noble men of the citie, and of all the places subiect vnto the same citie : who so soone as they came to speake with the captayne of the Spa-niardes, were incontinent apprehended before that anye bodye might perceiue the matter, to bee able therevppon to beare ty-dinges thereof vnto others. Then were demaunded of them fiue or sixe thousande Indians, to carry the loadings and carria-ges of the Spaniardes : which Indians came forth with, and were bestowed into the base courtes of the Housen. It was a pitifull case to see these poore folke, what time they made them redy to beare the carriages of the Spaniarde. They come all naked, onely their secrete partes couered, hauing euery one vp-on their shoulder a nette with a small deale of victuall : they bowe them selues euery one, and hold their backes cowred down like a sort of silly lambes, presenting them selues to the swords, and thus being all assembled in the base court together with o-thers, one part of the Spanishe all armed, bestowe them selues at the gates to hemme them in, whiles the rest put these poore sheepe to the edge of the sworde and the speares, in such sort, that there coulde not scape away one onely person, but that hee was cruelly put to death : sauing that after a two or three dayes, you might haue seene come forth sundry all couered with blood whiche had hid and saued them selues vnder the dead bodies of their fellowes, and nowe presenting them selues before the Spaniardes, asking them mercy and the sauing of their liues : they founde in them no pitie, nor compassion any whit at all, but were all hewed in peeces.

All the Lordes whiche were aboue and vnderneath, were all bounde, the Captayne commaunding them to bee brent quicke being bounde vnto stakes pitched into the grounde. Howebeit one Lorde, which might bee peraduenture the principall and king of the countrey saued him selfe, and cast him selfe with thirtie or fourtie other menne into a temple thereby, which was as good vnto them as a forte, whiche they call in their language, qewe : and there he defended him selfe a good part of the day. But the Spaniards, whose handes nothing can escape specially armed for the warre, cast fire on the temple, and burked all those which were within. Who cast out these voyces and cries, O yee euill men! O ye euill men! What displeasure haue wee done you? why doe yee slay vs? Goe, Goe you shall come at Mexico : where our Soueraigne Lorde Mortensuma shall take vengeance of you. It is reported that as the Spaniardes played this gay play in the base court, putting to the edge of the sword a fiue or sixe thousand men, their captaine hauing his heart all in a Iollitie sang.

Mira Nero de Tarpeya á Roma como se ardias
Gritos, dan ninos, y vieios : y el de nada se dolia:

That is to say,

Fro Tarpey top, dan Nero gan see Roome all flaming
   brenne,
Both young and old cry out, the whiles his heart did neuer
   yerne.

They made also another great butcherie in the Citie of Tapeaca : whiche was greater and of more number of householdes,

holdes, and more people inhabiting then in the citie afore sayde. They slue here with the sharpe of the sword, an infinite number of people, with great circustances & particularities of cruelties.

From Cholula they went to Mexico. The king Motensuma sent to meete them a thousande of presentes, and Lordes, and people, making ioy and mirth by the way.

And at the entry of the cawsie of Mexico, whiche reacheth two leagues in length, he sent also his brother, accompanied with a great number of honorable Lordes, bearing with them rich presents, gold, siluer, & apparell: & at the barres of the citie, the king in person with all his great court, came to receiue them, beeing carried in a lighter of golde, and them accompanied vnto the palace which hee had caused to bee made ready for them.

The selfe same very day, as some haue tolde me, the which were then and there present, they tooke by a certayne dissimulation the great king Motensuma, as he mistrusted nothing, and ordained fourescore men to keepe him. Afterwardes, they put giues on his feete. But letting all this passe, in the which there were notable poyntes to speake of, I will onely rehearse one which was singuler wrought by those tirantes. The Captaine general of the Spanishe was gone to the sea porte to take another Spanishe Captayne, which came against in warre: and hauing lefte another vnder captayne in his roome, with a fewe more then an hundreth men to keepe the sayde king Motensuma: these same aduised with them selues to doe another thing woorthy the note, to the ende, to encrease and augment more and more in all those regions, the awe which they had of them: a practise and stratageme which (as I sayde before) they haue often vsed. All this meane while the Indians, the common people, and the Lordes of the whole Citie sought none other thing, saue onely to shewe pleasure and pastime to their Lorde which was deteyned prisoner. And amongest other sportes which they made him: were their friskes and daunces whiche they made in the euening thorowe out all the high streetes and markette places, which daunces, they call Mitotes, as in the iles they call them Areytos.

The do weare in these friskes all their riche furniture, their best gorgious attyre, and their iewels, despising them selues to
                                                                                    liking

liking in all thinges, for these are the greatest signes of ioy and festiuitie that they doe vse. Nowe at this time, the nobilitie also, and princes of the blood royall, eche one after his degree kept their reuels and feastes at the neerest vnto the house where was deteyned prisoner their soueraigne. Ioyning vnto the walles of the saide palace, were there more then two thousande youthes, Lordes children, which were the flower of the nobilitie of all the state of Motensuma. Against those made out the captayne of the Spaniardes with a troupe of souldiers, sending the others vnto other places of the citie where the friskes and daunces were kept, and all making wise onely to go see them. The captayne had giuen in charge, that at a certayne appointed houre, they should all cast them vpon those dauncers, and hee himself for his own part, casting himselfe into the thronge, the Indians mistrusting nothing, but onely intending their disport, hee saith: Saynct Iago, let vs amongst them, & vpon thē sirs. And thus their arming swordes in their fistes, they began to rip these bodies naked and delicate, and to shed that blood gentle and noble, in such sort, as that they left not a man aliue. The others performed the like in other places, a thing which set all those realmes and nations in a fright & extreme desperation, and whereof as long as the world shall last, they will neuer lin (if themselues do not decay) to lament, and recorde in their Areytos & solemne meetings, as in rime these calamities, and the spoile of the spring of their ancient nobilitie, of the which they are wont to vaunt thēselues & glory very much.

The Indians seeing so great an iniquitie, and a crueltie neuer heard of the like, made against so many innocentes without any cause: specially hauing put vp quietly the imprisonment & that no lesse wrongfull of their soueraigne Lorde, who also had commaunded them not to make warre vpon the Spaniardes: all the citie put them selues in armes, wherevpon the Spaniards being assaulted and many of them hurt, with much a do might they escape, but set a dagger on the chest of the brest of the prisoner Motensuma to kill him, if he laied not him selfe out at a gallery or windowe, to cōmand the Indians that they should not beset the house, & they should keepe thē quiet. The Indians taking no care as then of obeying, aduised thē to chuse a L. & captayn from

amongst

amongst them selues to conduct their battals. And for as much
as the Captayn which was gone to the hauen, was returned vic-
torious, leading with him more Spaniardes then he had carried
foorth, and for that hee was nowe neere at hande, the combate
ceased about a three or foure dayes, vntill such time as hee was
entred the towne.

    Then the Indians assembled an infinite number of people
out of all the countrey, and skirmished in such wise, and so long
a season, that the Spanish thought they should al die on the place,
wherefore they deliberated to abandon the citie for one night.
That which their disseighu being knowen to the Indians, they
slewe of them a great number vppon the bridges of the Marshes
in a warre most rightfull, and most lawfull for the causes most
righteous which they had as hath been saide: the whiche euery
reasonable and true dealing man will mayneteyne for good.
Soone after, the Spanishe hauing realied them selues, the
combat with the Citie renewed, where the Spaniardes made an
horrible and ghastly butcherie of the Indians, and slue an infinite of people, and brent aliue the great Lords.

    After these great and abhominable tyrannies committed
in the Citie of Mexico, and in other cities, and the countrey
tenne, fifteene, and twentie leagues compasse of Mexico: this
tyrannie and pestilence aduaunced it selfe forwarde, to waste also, infect, and lay desolate the prouince of Panuco. It was a
thing to bee wondered at of the worlde, of people that there
were, and the spoyles and slaughters there done. Afterwarde
they wasted also after the selfe maner, all the prouince of Tutte-
peke, and the prouince of Ipelingo, and the prouince of Columa:
eche prouince conteyning more grounde then the realme of Leon & of Castile. It shoulde bee a thing very difficulte, yea, impossible to speake or recount the discomfitures, the slaughters, and
the cruelties, which they there committed: and woulde cause a
great remorse vnto the hearers.

    Here is to be noted, that the title wherewith they entred,
and begynne to make hauocke of all these harmelesse and silly
Indians, and haue dispeopled that countrey, which shoulde haue
caused a great reioycing to all those which shoulde bee in trueth
christi-

Christians, beyng so peopled as they were: was to say that they shoulde come and put them selues in subiection, to serue the king of Spain, otherwise that they woulde kill them, or make them slaues. And those which came not incontinent to satisfie their demaundes so vniust, and did not put them selues into the handes of men so vniust, cruell, and beastly, they called them rebelles, as those which had lift vp them selues agaynst the kinges Maiestie, and for such they accused them to the king our soueraigne Lorde: the blinde vnderstandings of those which gouerned the Indians ; beeing not able to comprehende nor perceyue this much, which in their lawes is more cleerely taught then any other principle of Lawe, that is, that none can bee reputed a rebell, if first hee be not a subiect. Nowe let Christians, and those which haue any percepuerance consider with them selues, if suche cases can prepare and informe the mindes of any nations whatsoeuer liuing in their countrey in assurance, and not thinking to owe any thing to any person, hauing their owne naturall liege Lordes whom they serue and obey, suddenly to come and tell them tydings:

Put you vnder the obeysance of a king a stranger, whom ye neuer sawe, nor neuer hearde of before: otherwise knowe yee that wee will rent yee incontinent all to peeces, specially when it is knowen by experience that they doe it in deede as soone as it is but sayde. And that which is farre more frightfull, they take those, which doe yeelde them selues to obey, to put them into a moste grieuous bondage, in the whiche there are toyles incredible, and tormentes greater and of longer continuance then those same of them which are excuted by the swoorde, for in the ende they perishe, they, their wiues, their children, and their whole generation.

And put the case, that through the threates and frightes aforesaide, those peoples, or any others whosoeuer doe come to obey and acknowledge the dominion of a straunger king: doe not these blunderers see, being altogether benummed with ambition and deuelish couetousnes, that they winne not a mite of right, forasmuche as so it is, that it is caused vpon frightes and terrours which might bee able to make men the constantest and

E   the

the best aduised: and that by the lawes of nature, man, and God,it hath no moze force then a handfull of winde,to make any thing auaplable to any purpose whatsoeuer, sauing the punish-ment and obligation which abideth them in the bottom of hel. J passe ouer the losses and dammages which they doe to the king, when as they spoyle his realmes, and bzing to nought (as much as in them lyeth)all the right which they haue in the Jndies.

These are nowe the seruices, whiche the Spaniardes haue done,and as yet doe at this houre vnto the aforesaide kinges,and soueraigne Lozds,vnder the colour of this gallant title,so right-full,and so smoothly garnished.

This Captayne tyzaunt, with this gozgeous and pzetended title, dispatched two other Captaynes, as very tyzauntes and farre moze cruell, and lesse pitifull then him selfe, into greate realmes most flourishing,and most fertile, and full of people,-to witte,the realme of Guatimala, which lieth to the seawarde on the South side,and the same of Naco,and Honduras, otherwise called Guaymura,which coasteth on the sea on the Nozth side, confronting and confining the one with the other , thzee hun-dzed leagues distaunce from Mexico. Hee sent the one by land, and the other by sea: both the one and the other carried with them a maynie of trowpes to serue on hozsebacke and a foote.

J say the trueth, that of the mischieues which these two haue wzought , and pzincipally hee whiche went to Guati-mala (foz that other dyed soone after of an euill death,) there might be made a great booke,of so many villanies, of so manie slaughters, so many desolations, and of so many outrages and bzutishe vniustices , as were able to affright the age pzesent and to come.

Foz certayne this man surpassed all the others,pzesent,and gone befoze,in quantitie and in number, as well foz the absmi-nations whiche hee committed,as foz the peoples and countreys whiche he layde waste and desert. All the which thinges were infinite.

Hee which went by sea,committed exceeding pillinges,cruel-ties,& disozders amongst the people on the sea coast: befoze whõ some comming with pzesents from the realme of Pucatane whi-

che

che is the high way to ȳ aforesaid realme of Naco & Guatmura, towards the which they went: when he came vnto them he sente captaynes, & a many of men of armes through all that land, whiche went sacking, slaughtering, & destroying as many people as there were to be foud, & principally one, who with three hundred more, hauing mutined and rebelled, and setting himselfe into the countrey towardes Guatimala, went spoyling and burning all the towns that he found, in killing and robbing the people inhabitants of them. That which he did of a set purpose, in more then an hundred and twentie leagues of the land, to the end, that if any had sent after him, those which should come, shoulde finde the countrey dispeopled and debelled, and that they were so slain of the Indians, in reuenge of the dammages and spoiles by them made. After whome haue succeeded sundry others most cruell tyrantes, the which with their slaughters and dreadful cruelties, and by bringing the Indians into thraldrome, whom afterwards they soulde vnto those who carried them with their shippings of wine, garments, and other things, and by reason of the tyrannicall seruitude ordinary, since the yeere a thousande, fiue hundred, twentie foure, vntill the yeere 1535. haue layd waste those same prouinces and realmes of Naco and Honduras, the which resembled a paradise of pleasures: and were more peopled, frequented, and inhabited, then any countrey of the worlde: and nowe of late we comming a long thereby, haue seene them so dispeopled and destroied, that who so should see them, his heart would cleaue for sorrowe, ware he neuer so flintie.

They haue slaine within these eleuen yeeres, more then two Millions of soules, hauing not left in more then an hundreth leagues of the countrey square, but two thousande persons, whome they slay as yet dayly in the sayde ordinarie bondage.

Nowe let vs returne to write of the great tyraunt and Captayne, which went to Guatimala, (who, as hath been sayde, exceeded all the aforepassed, and is comparable to all those, which are at this day) from the prouinces neere to Merico, (according as him selfe wrote in a letter to the principall tyraunt whiche had sente him) distaunte from the realme of Guatimala 400. leagues, (keeping ȳ way by him traced) & as he went, slu, robbed,

burned,

burned and destroyed all the countrey, wheresoeuer he became, vnder the shadow of title aboue mentioned, saying: ᵽ they should submit themselues vnto thē, that is to say, vnto men so vnnatural, so wicked, and so cruell: in the name of the king of Spaine, who was vnto them vnknowen, and of whom they had neuer hearde speake: and the which those nations there esteemed more vniust and more cruell then they his men were. And the tyrauntes giuing vnto them no respect of time to deliberate, they fling vpon the poore folke , in a maner as soone as the message was done, putting all to fire and blood.

Of the Prouince and realme
of Guatimala.

NO sooner arriued hee into this saide realme : but that he beganne with great slaughter of the inhabitaunces. This notwithstanding the chiefe Lorde came to receiue him, being caried in a lighter, with trumpettes and tabours, reioycinges, and disportes, accompanied with a great number of the Lordes of the citie of Vtlatan, head citie of the whole realme, dooing them also seruice with all they had, but specially in giuing them foode abundantly, ᵻ whatsoeuer they demaunded besids. The Spanish lodged this night without the citie, forasmuche as the same seemed vnto them strong, and there might bee thereby daunger.

This Captayne called to him the next morrowe the chiefe Lorde, with other great Lordes, who beeing come as meeke sheepe, hee apprehended them al, ᵻ commaunded thē to giue ʜim certayne summes of golde. They answering that they had none, forasmuch as the countrey yeelded none : hee commaundeth incontinent to burne them aliue , without hauing committed any crime whatsoeuer, and without any other forme of proces or sentence.

As the Lordes of all these prouinces perceiued , that they had burned their soueraigne Lordes, onely because they gaue them no golde, they fledde all to the mountaynes, commaunding
their

their subiectes to goe to the Spaniardes, and to serue them as their Lordes, but that they should not discouer them, nor giue the intelligence where they were.

With this, loe all the people of the countrey, presenting them, and protesting to bee theirs, and to serue them as their Lordes: The Captayne made answere that hee woulde not accept of them, but that hee woulde kill them if they tolde not where were their Lordes. The Indians answered, they could not tell ought: but as touching them selues they were content, that they shoulde employ them to their seruice, with their wiues and children: and that they should vse their housen, and that there they might kill, or doe what so euer them pleased.

It is a wonderfull thing, that the Spaniardes went to their villages and borrowes, and finding there these silly people at their worke, with their wiues and children, neyther misdoubting any thing they pearsed them with their Borespeares, and hackled them to peeces. They came to one borrowe great & mightie, which helde it selfe more assured then any other, because of their innocencie: whome the Spanishe layde desolate in a maner all whole, in the space of two houres, putting to the edge of the sword, children, with women, and aged persons, and all those which could not escape by flying.

The Indians seeing that by their humilitie, by their presentes and patience, they could not pacifie nor mitigate the madmoode, and enraged heartes of their enemies, and that without any reason, or shewe of reason, they were hackt in peeces: and seeing likewise that they were sure to die ere long: they deuised to assemble and realye themselues to die all in warre, and auenge themselues the best that they could vpon enemies so cruel and diuelishe: knowing also well enough them selues without weapons, starke naked, weake, and on foote, and suche as coulde by no meanes preuaple or carrie away the victory, but that in the ende they shoulde be destroyed: they aduised between them to digge certayne ditches in the middest of the wayes, to make their horses tomble into, and pearcing their bellies with pikes sharpned and brent at one ende, there bestowed of purpose, and couered ouer so orderly with greene turfe, that it seemed

C3   there

there was no such matter.

There fell in horses once or twise : for the Spaniardes afterwardes coulde beware of them. But nowe to auenge them, they made a law, that as many Indians as might be taken aliue, shoulde bee flong into the same pittes. Hereupon they cast in women with child, and women newe deliuered of childbirth, and olde folke as many as they coulde come by, vntyll that the ditches were filled vp. It was a lamentable thing to beholde the women with their children stabbed with these pickes. All besides, they slue with thrust of speares, and edge of swoorde. They cast of them also to flesche fraunching dogges, which tare them and deuoured them. They brent a Lord at a great fire of quicke flames : saying, they woulde herein doe him honour. And they persisted in these butcheries so vnnaturall, about seuen yeeres, from the yeere 24. vntill the yeere 31. Let any esteeme, what may bee the number of people : whome they might haue slayne.

Amongst an infinite of horrible actes which this cursed tyraunt did in this realme with his bandes of souldiers, (for his vnder captaynes were no lesse mischieuous and insensate then himselfe, and withall likewise those that were vnder them again to serue their turne,) this one was notable: That where as in the prouince of Cuzcatan, where is at this houre, or neere there aboutes the citie of Saint Sauiour, a countrey very fertile with all the sea coaste on the Southe, contayning fourtie or fiftie leagues : and likewise in the Citie of Cuscatan the mother Citie of the prouince, there had been made him a very great entertaynement, of more then twentie or thirtie thousande Indians attending him, all laden with poultrie and other victuals : this Captayne arriuing, and hauing receiued the presentes, hee commaunded that euery one of the Spaniardes shoulde take of this great number of people, such as shoulde please him, to serue him all the time that they shoulde make their abode there, and that they shoulde constrayne them to beare for them, of their carriage all that should bee needefull.

Euery man tooke vnto him other an hundred, or fiftie, or as many

many as it feemed fuffiled him to bee well ferued. Thefe poore lambelikeinnocentes ferued the Spaniards with all their power, that there wanted nothing, vnleffe they fhoulde doe vnto them godly honour. Meane while this captayne demaunded of the Lordes very much golde: for they were principally commen for that purpose.

The Indians anfweredthat they were ready to giue them all the golde they had : and layed together a great furniture of hatchets of copper and gylt, where with they ferue their owne turnes,the same refembling golde, as in deede it hath in it some litle deale. The Captayne cauſeth to put to the touch: and as he ſawe it was copper,hee ſayde to the Spaniardes, nowe the diuell take ſuch a countrey: let vs bee gone hence,ſeeing here is no golde heere:and euery man put the Indians whiche hee hath retayned to ſerue him, to the hotte irons, and ſo to marke them for ſlaues.

That which they did, branding with the kinges marke all that they might. I ſawe the ſonne him ſelfe ofthe principall Lorde of this citie,to bee ſo branded. The Indians which eſcaped,with all other of the Countrey ſeeing all the miſchieſes of the Spaniſhe, beganne to aſſemble, and put them ſelues in armes : wherevppon the Spaniardes woorke great diſcomfitures and ſlaughters,returning to Guatimala where they builded a citie, the which God of a iuſt iudgement hath renuerſed with three ouerwhelmings falling all three together : the one was with water,the other with earth,and the thirde with ſtones, of the bigneſſe oftenne or twentie oxen. By ſuche like meanes all the Lordes and the men that were able to beare armes being ſlayne : thoſe which remayned, were reduced into the diabolicall ſeruitude aforeſaide,being made tributary ſlaues or villayns regardant, but giuing for their tribute ſonnes and daughters, for they will haue none other kind of bondmen.And ſo the Spaniards ſending whole ſhips laden with them to Peru to ſell the, with their other ſlaughters,haue deſtroyed & laide deſert an whole

realme

Realme of an hundred leagues square or aboue, a countrey the most blessefull, and peopled the most that might be in the worlde.

For the tyraunt him selfe wrote hereof, that it was more peopled then Mexico : and herein hee sayde the trueth. Hee hath done to death, with his consortes and confrayryes, more then foure or fiue Millions of soules in fifteen or sixteen yeeres space, from the yeere twentie foure, vnto the fourtieth yeere : and yet at this houre they slay and destroy those that remayne.

This tyraunt had a custome, when as hee went to make warre vpon any Citie or Prouince : to carrie thither of the Indians alreadie vnder yoked, as many as hee coulde, to make warre vpon the other Indians : and as hee gaue vnto a ten or twentie thousande men which he ledde along no sustenaunce, he allowed them to eate the Indians whiche they tooke: And so by this meanes hee had in his campe an ordinarie shambles of mans fleshe, where, in his presence they killed and roasted children. They killed men, onely to haue off from them their handes and their feete, which partes they helde to be the dayntiest morcels. When the nations of other countreys vnderstoode of all those vnnaturall doings, they coulde not tel what to do for frightfulnesse.

He was the death of an infinite sorte of the Indians in making of shippes, the which hee carried from the North sea vnto the South, which are an hundred and thirtie leagues. He transported after this rate great store of artillerie, which he loded vpon the shoulders of these poore folke going naked: whereby I haue seene very many fall downe in the high way, by reason of their great burdens.

Hee vndid whole housholdes, by taking from the men their wiues and daughters : the which afterwardes hee dispersed in gyftes to his marriners and souldiers to please them withall, who led them along with them in their nauies. He stuffed all the shippes with Indians, where they dyed for thyrst and hungar. Certaynely if I shoulde stande to tell the particularities of thise cruelties : I shoulde make a great booke thereof, whiche shoulde astonishe the worlde. Hee made two nauies, eyther of

a

a great number of shippes, with the which hee consumed as with fire and lightning flashing from heauen all those peoples : Oh howe many poore children hath hee made fatherlesse Orphans, howe many men and women widowers and widowes, bereeuing thē also of theirchildrē? How many adulteries, whoredoms and rapes, hath he been the cause of! How many hath he of free made villanyes : Howe many anguishes and calamities by him haue nombers suffered : Howe many hath hee caused to shedde teares, sighes and groninges : Of how many desolations hath he been the occasion in this life, and the meanes for others to fall into euerlasting damnation in the life to come, not onely of the Indians which are innumerable, but of the miserable Spaniardes, with whose ayde he hath serued himselfe in villanies so excessiue, and sinnes so enormous, and abominations so execrable: I wishe in God that hee had taken pitie of him: and that hee had been pleased in so euill an ende as he sent him.

Of newe Spaine, and Panuco, and Xalisco.

AFter the exceeding cruelties and slaughters aforesayd, and the others whiche I haue omitted, whiche haue been executed in the prouinces of newe Spayne and Panuco : there came to Panuco an other tyraunt, cruell, and vnbrideled, in the yeere 1525. Who in committing very many cruelties, and in branding many for slaues, after the maner aforesayde which were all free, and in sending very many shippes laden to Cuba, and Pispaniola, where they might best make Marchandise of them, hee atchieued the desolation of this prouince.

And it hath come to passe in his tyme, that there hath been giuen for one Mare eyght hundred Indians soules partakers of reason. And this man from this roome was promoted to bee president of Mexico, and of all the prouince of new Spaine, and there were promoted with him other tyrauntes, to the offices of Auditorshippes : in the which dignities they committed so many

F   vn-

vngracious turnes, so manie sinnes, so many cruelties, robberies, and abhominations, that a man can not beleeue them to be such. And they set forwarde also this countrey into so extreme a desolation, that if God had not kept them by meanes of the resistance of the religious men of Saint Francis order, and if that there had not been prouided with all speede a court of audience, and the kings counsayle in those partes friende to all vertue, they had laide wast all newe Spayne, as they haue done the Ile of Hispaniola.

There was a man, amongst those of the company of this captayne, who to the end to enclose a garde of his, w a wal: kept in his workes eight thousande Indians, without paying them ought, nor giuing them to eate, in maner that they dyed, falling down suddely, & he neuer tooke the more thought for the matter.

After that the chiefe Captayne which I spake of, had finished the laying waste of Panuco, and that hee vnderstoode the newes of the comming of the kinges court of Audience: hee aduised with him selfe to proceede farther, into the innermoste partes of the realme, to search where hee might tyrannize at his ease, and drewe by force out of the prouince of Mexico 15. or 20. Millions of men, to the ende, that they shoulde carrie the loades and carriages of the Spaniardes whiche went with him, of whom there neuer returned agayne two hundred, the others being dead on the high wayes.

Hee came at the prouince of Mechuacam, which is distant from Mexico fourtie leagues, a region as blissefull and full of inhabitauntes, as is that of Mexico. The king and Lorde of the countrey went to receiue him with an infinite companie of people, which did vnto them a thousande seruices and curtisies

Hee apprehended him by and by, for that hee had the brute to be very rich of gold and siluer: and to the ende, that hee shoulde giue him great treasures, hee beganne to giue him the torments, and put him in a payre of stockes by the feete, his body stretched out, and his handes bounde to a stake, hee maketh a flashing fire against his feete, and there a boy with a basting sprinkle soked in oyle in his hande stoode and basted them a litle and a litle, to the ende to well roaste the skynne. There was in one side of him a cruell man; the whiche with a crossebowe bente, aymed ryght at his heart, on the other side an other which helde a dogge snarling, and leaping vp as to renne vppon him, which in lesse then the tyme of a Credo, had beene able to haue torne him in pieces: and thus they tormented him, to the ende hee shoulde discouer the treasures which they desired, vntyll suche tyme as a religious man of Saint Fraunces order tooke him away from them, notwithstanding that hee dyed of the same tormentes.

They tormented and slue of this fashion very many of the Lordes and Cacikes in these Prouinces: to the ende that they shoulde giue them gold and siluer.

At the same time a certayne tyrant going in visitation to visite the powches, and to robbe the godes of the Indians, more then for any care hee had of theyr soules, founde, that certayne Indians had hid their Idolles, as those which had neuer been better instructed by y cursed Spaniards of any better god, he apprehended and detayned prisoners the Lordes, vntyll suche time as that they woulde giue them their Idolles: Supposing all this while they had beene of golde or of siluer: Howebeit they were not so, wherefore hee chastised them cruelly and vniustly.

But to the ende hee woulde not remayne frustrate of his intent, which was to spoyle, hee constrayned the Cacikes to redeeme their sayde Idolles, and they redeemed them for such gold & siluer as they coulde find, to the ende, to worship them for Gods, as they had bin wont to do aforetime. These be the examples & deedes which these cursed Spaniardes do: and this is the honour which they purchase to God, amongst the Indians.

This great tyraunt and Captayne passed farther from Mechuacham to the Prouince of Xalisco, the which was all whole most full of people, and most happie. For it is one of the moste fertillest and most admirable countrey of the Indies, whiche had borrowes containing in a maner seue leagues. As he entred this coūtrey the L. with y inhabitants, according as al y Indians are accustomed to do, wēt to receiue hun wt presēts & ioyfulnes. Hee begā to cōmit his cruelties & mischieuousnes, wt he had learned & all the rest had bin accustomed to practise, wt is to heap vp gold wt is their god. He burned townes, he tooke y Cacikes prisonners, and gaue them torments. Hee made slaues all that hee tooke.

F 2   Where

whereof there died an infinite number tyed in chaynes.   The women newe deliuered of childebyrth , going laden with the stuffe of euill Christians, and being not able to beare their owne children because of trauell and hunger, were fayne to cast them from them in the wayes, whereof there dyed an infinite.

An euill Christian taking by force a young Damsell to a-buse her, the mother withstoode him : and as shee woulde haue taken her away, the Spaniarde drawing his dagger or rapier, cutte off her hande, and slue the young gyrle with slashes of his weapon: because shee woulde not consent to his appetite.

Amongst manye other thinges , hee caused vniustly to bee marked for slaues , foure thousande, fiue hundred soules as free as they, men, women, and sucking babes, from of a yere and a halfe olde, vnto three or foure peeres olde: which notwithstan-ding had gone before them in peace, to receiue them with an infi-nite number of other thinges that haue not beene set downe in writing.

Hauing atchieued the diuelishe warres innumerable , and hauing in the same committed very many slaughters, hee redu-ced all that countrey into the ordinary seruitude, pestilential and tyrannicall, into the which all the tyrant Spaniardes whiche are in the Indies, are accustomed, or pretende to cast those people. In the which countrey, hee consented also, and permitted his Ste-wardes and all others to execute tormentes neuer hearde of be-fore, to the ende, to drawe from the Indians golde and tribute. His Stewardes slewe very many of the Indians, hanging them and burning them aliue, and casting some vnto the dogges, cut-ting off their feete, handes, head, and tongue, they being in peace, onely to bring them into a feare, to the ende they shoulde serue him, and giue him golde and tributes: all this knowing, and see-ing this gentle tyrant , euen to come to the whippes , basto-nads, blowes, with other sorts of cruelties wherewith hee vexed and oppressed them dayly.

It is sayde of him, that hee hath destroyed and burned in this realme of Xalisco, eyght hundred borroughes, whiche was the cause that the Indians being fallen desperate , and seeing those which remayned, howe they perished thus cruelly ; they lift vp

them-

themselues, and went into the mountaynes, slaying certayne Spaniardes: howe be it by good right. And afterwardes because of the wickednesses and outrages of other tyrauntes now being, which passed by that way to destroy other prouinces (that which they call discouering) many of the Indians assembled, fortifiyng them selues vpon certayne rockes. Upon the whiche rockes the Spanishe haue made, and yet at this present, and a freshe doe make so many cruelties, that they almost made an end of slaying desolate all this great countrey , slaying an infinite number of people.

And the wretched blunderers forsaken of God , and giuen ouer into a reprobate sense, not seeing the causes most iust which the Indians haue by the lawes of nature, man, and God, to hew them in peeces, if they had strength and muniinentes, and so to cast them out of their countrey : and not seeing the wickednes of their owne cause, ouer and besids so many violents and tyrannies which they haue committed in that sort , to mooue warre a newe : they thinke, speake, and write of the victories which they haue ouer the poore Indians , leauing them in desolation, that it is G O D which giueth the same vnto them, as though their warres were atchieued rightfully: thus they reioyce, vaunt themselues, and giue thankes vnto God for their tyrannies, as did those tyrantes and theeues of whom speaketh the Prophete Zacharie, in the eleuenth chapter: verse 4. saying:

Feede the sheepe of the slaughter , they that possesse them slay them, and are not grieued, and they that sell them, say , blessed be the Lorde, for we are become rich.

Of the realme of Yuca-
tan.

THe yeere one thousande, fiue hundred, twentie and sixe, was deputed ouer the Realme of Yucatan an other captife gouernour, and that through the lies and false reports which himselfe had made vnto the king : in like maner as hath the other tirantes,

rants vntill this present, to the end there might bee committed
vnto thee offices & charges, by means wherof they might rob at
their pleasures. This realme of Yucatan was full of inhabitants: for that it was a countrie in euery respect holsome, and
abounding in plentie of victuals, and of fruites more then Mexico: and singulerly exceeded for the aboundance of honnie and
waxe there to bee founde, more then in any quarter of the Indies, which hath beene seene vnto this present. It conteyneth
about three hundred leagues compasse. The people of that countrie, were the most notable of all the Indies, as well in consideration of their policie and prudencie, as for the vprightnes of their
life, verily worthie the training to the knowledge of God: a-
mongest whome there might haue beene builded great Cities,
by the Spanishe, in which they might haue liued as in an earth-
ly Paradise, if so bee they had not made themselues vnworthie,
because of their exceeding couetousnesse, harde heartednes,
and heynous offences: as also vnworthie they were of other
moe blessings a great many, which God had set open in these
Indies. This tyrant began with three hundred men to make
warre vpon these poore innocent people, which were in their
houses without hurting any body: where he slue and ransacked
infinite numbers. And for because the Countrie yeeldeth no
golde, for if it had yeelded any, hee woulde haue consumed those
same Indians, in making them to toyle in the mynes: to the
ende hee might make golde of the bodies and soules of those
for whome Iesus Christe suffered death, hee generally made
slaues of all those whome hee slue not, and returned the ships
that were come thither, vpon the blowing abrode and noyse of
the selling of slaues, ful of people bartered for wine, oyle, vinegar, powdred Bacons fleshe, garments, horses, and that, that e-
uery man had neede of, according to the Captaines estimate
and iudgement. Hee woulde let choose amongest an hundred
or fiftie young Damosels: barterting some one of the fayrest, &
of the best complexion, for a caske of wine, oyle, vinegar, or for
a porke powdred. And in like maner hee woulde let choose out
a young handsome stripling amongst two or three hundreth for
the

the aforesaide merchandize. And it hath beene seene, that a youth seeming to be ý sonne of some prince, hath been bartered for a Cheese, and an hundreth persons for an horse. Hee continued in these voinges from the yeere twentie sixe, vntill the yeere thirtie three, which are seuen yeeres, desolating and dispeopling those Countries, and killing the people there without pitie or mercie, vntill the time that the newes came of the riches of Peru, and that thereupon the Spaniardes hyed them thither, by occasion whereof this Diuelish tyrannie ceased for a season. A few dayes after, his men returned, to doe and commit other haynous enormities, as robberies, & wrongful imprisonments, with offences great against God: neither doe they cease as yet at this day to doe them, but haue laide desart and dispeopled all those three hundred leagues, the which were as well replenished and peopled, as hath been saide.

There is no man that can beleeue, or rehearse the cases particuler of the cruelties. which were of them committed. I wyll onely rehearse two or three, comming to my remembraunce at this instant. As these cursed Spaniards, went with their mad dogges a foraging by the tracke, and hunting out the Indian men and women: An Indian woman beeing sicke, and seeing shee coulde not escape their dogges, that they shoulde not rent her as they did others: shee tooke a corde and hanged herselfe at a beame, hauing fastened at her foote a childe shee had of a yeere olde, and shee had no sooner done: beholde these Curres, whiche come and dispatche this infante, howe beit that before it dyed, a Religious man a Fryar baptized it.

When the Spanishe parted out of this Realme, one amongest others saide, to a sonne of a' Lorde of some Citie or Prouince, that hee shoulde goe with him: the boy aunswered, and sayde, hee woulde not forsake his Countrie. The Spaniarde replyed: Goe with mee, or els I will cutte off thine eares. The young Indian persisted in his first saying, that hee woulde not forsake his Countrie. The Spaniarde drawing out his dagger, cut off first one, & then his other eare.

The

The young man abyding by it ſtill that hee woulde not leaue his countrey: hee mangled off alſo his noſe, with the vppermoſt of his lippes: making no moꝛe ſcrupuloſitie of the matter, then if hee had giuen him but a phillip.

This damnable wꝛetch magnified him ſelfe, and vaunted him of his doynges villauouſly vnto a reuerende religious perſon, ſaying: that hee tooke as much paynes as hee coulde, to begette the Indian women in great numbers with childe, to the ende, hee might receiue the moꝛe money foꝛ them in ſelling them great with childe foꝛ ſlaues.

In this realme, oꝛ in one of the pꝛouinces of newe Spaine, a certayne Spaniard went one day with his dogs on hunting of veniſon, oꝛ els conies, and not finding game, hee minded his dogs that they ſhould be hungrie, and tooke a little ſweet Babie which hee bereaued the mother of, and cutting off from him the armes, and the legges, chopped them in ſmall gobbettes, giuing to euery dog his liuery oꝛ part thereof, by ꝓ by after theſe moꝛſels thus diſpatched, hee caſt alſo the reſt of the body oꝛ the carkaſe to all the kenell together.

By this ye may ſee how great the dull heartednes of the Spaniardes is in that countrey, and howe God hath deliuered them vp into a repꝛobate ſenſe: and what accoumpt they make of thoſe ſame nations which are created after the image of God, and redeemed with the blood of his Chꝛiſt. We ſhal ſee hereafter moꝛe notable matter.

Leauing nowe the cruelties infinite, and neuer hearde of the like, which in this realme were done by thoſe which call thē ſelues Chꝛiſtians, and ſuch as no iudgement of man can ſufficiently imagine them: I will conclude with this ſame: That is, that being nowe departed the realme all the diueliſh tyꝛantes, blynded with the couetouſnes of the riches of Peru. ꝑ reuerend father, fryer Iames, with foure other religious of S. Frauncis, was moued in ſpirice to goe into this realme to pacifie them, and foꝛ to pꝛeach to them, and to win vnto Ieſus Chꝛiſt thoſe which might bee remayning of the butcheries and tyꝛannous murders, which the Spaniſh had bin perpetrating ſeuen continuall yeres.

And I beleeue that theſe ſame were thoſe religious perſons, the

the which in the yeere 34. certaine Indians of the Prouince of Mexico, sending before them messengers in their behalf, requested them that they woulde come into their countrie, to giue thē knowledge of that one onely God, who is God, and very Lorde of all the worlde : and for whose occasion the Indians helde a councell sundrie times, parlementing and informing themselues in their folke motes : to wit, what kinde of men those might be, which were called by the speciall name of fathers and brethren, and what it was that they pretended, and wherein they differed from the Spaniardes, of whom they had receiued so many outrages and iniuries : according in the ende to admit them with condition, that they should enter themselues alone, and not the Spaniardes with them, that which the religious promised thē. For it was permitted them, yea, commaunded them so to doe, by the Uiceroy of new Spaine, and that there shoulde no kinde of displeasure bee done vnto them by the Spaniardes. The Religious men preached vnto them the Gospell of Chryste, as they are accustomed to doe, and as had been the holy intention of the kinges of Castile, that shoulde haue beene done . Howbeit, that the Spaniardes in all the seuen yeres space past, had neuer giuen thē any such notice of the truth of the Gospel, or so much as that there was any other king sauing himself, ȳ so tyrannised ouer them, and destroyed them. By these meanes of the religious, after the ende of fortie dayes that they had preached vnto them, the Lordes of the countrie brought vnto them, and put into their handes their idols, to the end that they shoult burne them. After also, they brought vnto them their young children , that they should catechise them, whom they loue as the apple of their eye. They made for them also Churches, and Temples, and houses. Moreouer, some other prouinces sent , and inuited them, to the ende that they might come to them also, to preache, and giue them the vnderstandiug of God, and of him whom they saide to be the great king of Castile. And beeing perswaded and induced by the religious, they did a thing which neuer yet before hath been done in the Indies. (For whatsoeuer the tyrants, some of those which haue spoyled those Realmes, & great Countries, haue contriued to blemishe and defame the poore In-

G   DIANS

dians withall, they are mockeries and leasings:) twelue or fifteene Lordes, which had very many subiecets and great dominion, assembling euery one for his owne part his people, and taking their aduise and consent, of their owne voluntarie motion, yeelded themselues to the subiection, and to bee vnder the domination of the kinges of Castile: admitting the Emperour as king of Spain, for their liege Soueraigne. Wherof also they made certaine instrumentes, by them consigned, which I keepe in my charge, together with the testimonies thercunto of the said religious.

The Indians being thus onwarde in the way of the faith, with the great ioy, and good hope of the Religious brethren, that they shoulde bee able to winne vnto Iesus Christe all the people of the Realme that were the residue, beeing but a smal number of the slaughters, and wicked warres passed: There entred at a certaine coaste, eighteene Spaniarde tyrantes on horse backe, and twelue on foote, driuing with them great loades of Idols, which they had taken in the other Prouinces of the Indians. The Captaine of those thirtie Spaniards, called vnto him a Lorde of the countrie there aboutes as they were entred, and commaundeth him to take those idols; and to disperse them throughout al his countrie, selling euery idol for an Indian mā, or an Indian woman, to make slaues of them, with threatening them, that if hee did not doe it, hee woulde bidde them battaile. That saide Lorde beeing forced by feare, distributed those Idols throughout all the countrie, and commaunded all his subiectes, that they should take them to adore them, and that they shoulde returne in exchaunge of that ware Indies and Indisses to make slaues of. The Indians beeing affeard, those which had two children, gaue him one, and he that had three gaue him two. This was the ende of this sacrilegious trafficke: and thus was this Lord or Cacick, faine to content these Spaniards: I say not Christians.

One of these abhominable chafferers, named Iohn Garcia, beeing sicke, and neere his death, had vnder his bed two packs of Idols, and commaunded his Indish maide that serued him,

to

to looke to it that she made not away his idols, that there were
for Murlimeus, for they were good stuffe : and that making
vent of them, she should not take lesse then a slaue for a peece
one of them with another: and in fine, with this his Testament and last will thus deuised, the caytife dyed, busied with
this deep goodly care, and who doubteth but that he is lodged in
the bottome of hell:

Let it nowe bee considered, and well weyed, what kinde of
aduauncement of religion it is, and what are the good examples
of Christianitie of the behalfe of the Spanishe, that sayle to
the Indies? What honour they doe vnto God, how they paine
themselues to haue him knowen and adored of those nations:
what carke and care they haue of the doing of it, that by their
meanes the rather the sacred faith shoulde bee dispersed, en-
creased, and enlarged in the free passage thereof, amongest
those silly creatures? And let it with all bee discerned, if the
sinne of these men be any whit lesse then the same of *Ieroboam*,
Which made Israel to sinne, by making two golden Calues
for the people, to fall downe before, and worshippe: or otherwise
if it bee not like to the treason of Iudas, and which hath caused
more offence.

These bee the iestes of the Spaniardes, whiche goe to tye
Indies, whiche of a truth very many times, yea, an infinit sort
of times, for couetyse, and to scratche golde, haue solde and do
sell: haue reneaged, and do reneage as yet hitherto, and at this
present day: Christ Iesus.

The Indians perceiuing that, that, which the religious
had promised them, was as good as nothing : namely, that
the Spaniardes shoulde not enter those Prouinces : and seeing the Spaniards whiche had laded thither idols from other
places, there to make vent of them, they hauing put al their idols
afore into the handes of the Fryars, to the ende they shoulde bee
burned, and to the ende the true God shoulde bee by them adored, all the Countrie was in a mutinie, and a rage a-
gainst the religious Fryars, and the Indians comming vnto
them, say:

Why

Why haue you lyed vnto vs, in promising vs by deceites that there should not enter any Spaniardes into these Countries? And why haue you burnt our gods, seeing the Spaniards doe bring vs other gods from other nations? Were not our gods as good, as the gods of other prouinces? The fryars pacified them in the best maner that they coulr, not knowing what to answere them: and went to seeke out those thirtie Spaniards, to whom they declared the euill which they had done, praying thē to get them thence. That which the Spaniards would not doe, but saide to the Indians, that those religious men had caused them to come thither themselues of their owne accorde, whiche was rightly an extreeme maliciousnesse. In the end the Indians deliberated to kill the religious men: By occasion whereof, the Fryars fled away in a night, hauing aduertisement of the case by some of the Indians. But after that they were gone, the Indians better informed of the innocencie of the religious mē, and of the vngraciousnesse of the Spaniardes, the sent messengers after them, neere hand fiftie leagues of, beseeching them to come againe, and crauing pardon of them. The religious, as the seruants of God, and zealous for the winning of their soules, beleeuing them, returned to them, and were receiued as it had been Angels. And the Indians doyng them a thousand seruires, abode with them foure or fiue monethes. And for because the Spaniards would neuer departe that Countrie, and that namely the Uiceroy with all that he could doe, could not draw them thence, newe Spaine beeing farre of, howbeit, hee had caused them to bee proclaimed traitours: And for as muche as they neuer ceased to commit their outrages, and griefes accustomed amongst the Indians, the religious perceiuing that sooner or later they should smell of the smoke, and peraduenture the euill light vpon their heades: and specially that they coulde not preach vnto the Indians with quiet, and assurance of the Indias, & of themselues, by reason of the continuall assaultes and lewde deportments of the Spanish, they deliberated to leaue ẏ realme: Which in this maner was destitute of the light and the doctrine: and those soules abode vnder the darknesse of ignorance, and in the miserie they were in, the remedie, and the watering of the

know

knowledge of God being bereaued them, alreadie euen at their best, and when as they began to receiue it with exceeding willingnes: altogether like as if one should withdraw the watring from tender plants, and new set into a drie ground, at a hot time of the yeere: and this by the cursed vngraciousnesse of the Spanish.

Of the Prouince of Saint
Martha.

THe prouince of Saint Martha, was a countrie where the Spaniardes gathered golde in all plentie: the land beeing with the regions adiacent very rich, and the people industrious to drawe out the golde. Wherefore also from the yeere one thousand, fiue hundred, fortie two, infinite tyrants haue made thither continually with their ships, ouerrunning, and raunging along the countrie, killing and spoyling those the inhabitants, and ramping from them that gold that they had, with speedie returne euer to their ships, which went and came oftentimes. And so wrought they in those prouinces great wastes, and slaughters, and cruelties horrible, & that most commonly on the Sea coast, and certaine leagues within the countrie, vntill the yeere one thousand, fiue hundred, and three. At what time there wente Spanish tyrants to inhabite there. And for as much as the countrie was exceeding riche as hath been said, there euer succeeded Captaines one in anothers roome, euerie one more cruell then other: in such sort that it seemed that euerie one inforced himselfe, for the masterie in doing of euilles and cruelties more haynous then had been done by his predecessour. Wherefore herein is the rule verified that we haue giuen before. The yeere one thousande, fiue hundred, twentie and nine, there went a great tyrant, very resolute, with great troupes: but without any feare of God, or compassion of the nature of man, who wrought suche wastes, and slaughters so greate, that hee exceeded all others that had gone before him, himselfe robbing for

G 3

the

the space of sixe or seuen yeares that he lyued, great treasures : saue after bceing deceased without confession, and fledde from the place of his residence : there succeeded him other murdering tyrantes, and theeues, which made an ende of the rest of the people, whome the embrewed handes with blood, and the caruing swoordes of the tyrantes his forerunners, coulde not extyrp.

They set themselues so forwarde in the countrey, in inuading and laying desolate very manye prouinces, with killing, and taking prisoners those people, after the fashion before practised in other Prouinces, causing the Lordes together with their Subiectes to suffer grieuous torments, both to make them discouer the golde, and the places where golde might bee had : surmounting as is sayde euery way in number of mischieuous doinges, and in the maner of dooing, all that had passed before : that from the yeere one thousande, fiue hundred, twentie and niene, vnto this day, they haue reduced into a wildernesse in those same quarters more then foure hundred leagues of lande, which was no lesse peopled then the other countreys which wee haue spoken of.

Uerily if J had to make a bedrolle of the vngraciousnesses, of the slaughters, of the desolations, of the iniquities, of the violencies, of the massacres, and other greate insolencies whiche the Spaniardes haue done, and committed in those Prouinces of Saint Martha agaynst God, the king, and agaynst those innocent nations : J shoulde write an historie very ample. But that maye bee done if God spare mee lyfe, hereafter in his good tyme : onely J will sette downe a fewe woordes of that which was written in a letter by a Byshoppe of this Prouince to the king our Soueraigne : and the letter beareth date the twentieth of May, 1541. The whiche Byshoppe amongst other woordes, speaketh thus : J say, sacred Maiestie, that the way to redresse this countrey, is that his Maiestie deliuer her out of the power of Stepfathers, and giue vnto her an husbande whiche may intreate her as is reason, and according as shee deserneth : otherwise, J am sure hereafter as the tyrauntes whiche nowe haue the gouernement, doe torment and tormoyle her, shee will soone take an ende, &c.

And

And a little belowe hee sayeth : Whereby, your Maiestie shall knowe clearely, howe those whiche gouerne in those quarters doe deserue to bee disamounted , and deposed from their gouernment , to the ende, that the common weales maye bee relieued. That if that be not done , in mine aduise, they can neuer be cured of their diseases. His maiestie shal vnderstand moreouer, that in those regions, there are not any Christians but diuels, that there are no seruantes of God and the king, but traitors to the state, and their king. And in truth the greatest encombraunce that I finde in reducing the Indians, that are in warre, and to set them at peace, and to lead those which are at peace to the knowledge of our faith, is vnnaturall & cruell entreaty, which they that are in peace do receiue of the spanish, being so deeply altered, & lauced, that they haue nothing in more hatred & horror, then the name of christians, the which in al these countreys they cal in their laguage, yares, that is to say, diuels. For the acts which they comitted here, are neither of christians, nor of men which haue the vse of reaso: but of diuels. Whereof it commeth to passe, that the Indies which doe see these behauiors to be generally so far estraged fro all humanity, & without any mercy, aswell in the heads as in the mebers: they esteem, that the christians do hold these things for a law, & that their God, & their K. are the authors thereof. And to endeuor to perswad the otherwise, were to endeuor in vaine, & to minister vnto the the more ample matter, to deride and scorne Iesus Christ & his law. The Indians that are in warre , seeing the intreatie vsed toward the Indians that are in peace : woulde chuse rather to die once for all, then to endure sundrie deathes, beyng vnder the command of the Spanish. I knowe this by experience, most victorous Cesar. &c.

He sayth for a surcharge in a chapter a little lower, His M. hath in these parts more seruants then it supposeth. For here is not one souldier of so many as are of them, that dare not say openly & publikly, that if he roue, rob, wast, slay, or burne the subiects of his M. to the ende that they giue him some gold, he serueth there in your M. with this title, that he saith, therof redoundeth to his M. his part. Wherfore, most christia Cesar, it should be good, that your M. gaue them to vnderstand, by chastising some seuerely, that it

recei-

receiueth no seruice in ought, whereby God is disobeyed and dishonoured. All the abouesayde are the formall woordes of the saide Bishoppe of Saint Martha : by the which may bee seene clearly, what is done at this day amongest these poore innocent peoples in those countreys.

He calleth the Indians in warre, those which saued themselues by flying into the mountaines from the slaughters of the mischieuous Spaniardes. And hee calleth the Indians in peace, those which after hauing lost an infinite of their people , by the massacres, haue been thralled into the tyrannicall and horrible seruitude aforesayde, and whereof in the ende they haue been stoned out, desolated, and slayne, as appeareth by that which hath been saide by the Bishoppe, which notwithstanding speaketh but litle, in comparison of that which they haue suffered.

The Indians in that countrey haue accustomed to say , if when they are trauayled and dryuen vp the mountaynes loden, they happen to fall downe, and to fainte for feeblenesse, and for payne : for at that tyme they lay on vpon them blowes with their feete and with their staues , and they breake theyr teethe with the pomelles of their swordes, to make them rise , and march on without taking of breath, with these woordes, out vpon thee, what a villanie art thou: they (I say) the Indians, for their partes are wont to say, I can no more: kill mee heere right. I doe desire to die heere: and this they say with great sighes, and beeing scarce able to speake, for hauing their heart drawen together, declaring a great anguishe and dolour. But who were able to giue to vnderstande the hundreth parte of the afflictions and calamities, that these innocent people doe suffer of the cursed Spaniardes ? God make them to take knowledge of it, that are able and bounde to redresse it.

Of the Prouince of Cartha-
gene.

This Prouince of Carthagene is situate vnder, and a fiftie leagues distant from the same of Saint Martha, towardes the West , confining with the prouince of Ceu, vnto the gulph

of

of Araba: which are a hundred leagues all along the Sea side, and is a great countrie within land towardes the South. These Prouinces since the peere 1498. or 99. vntill nowe haue beene euill entreated, martyred, massacred, desolated like vnto that of Saint Martha: and there hath beene in these same done by the Spaniardes such cruelties, ransackinges, and pillagings enormous: as the which to make an ende the rather of this briefe Summarie, as also to make way to the rehearsall of their euill doinges in other Prouinces, I will not stande to touch in particuler.

Of the Coaste of Perles, and of
Paria, and of the Isle of the Trinitie.

FRom the coast of Paria, vnto the goulph of Venesuela, without foorth, which are two hundred leagues: the Spanishe haue wrought great and straunge destructions, rioting vppon that people, and taking aliue as many as they coulde, to the ende they might sell them for slaues: and oftentimes making them prisoners against the assurance and the promise of friendshippe made vnto them, neither keeping with them their faith plighted vnto them, the friendly entertainement which they had receiued of those good people notwithstanding: hauing beene entertained and entreated in their houses, as parents and children, vsing them to serue theirturn withall, and inioying all that they had, and that that they were able to doe for them. It cannot bee well told, nor particularly exprest, the sundrie kindes and greeuous vexations, wronges, hurtes, and spoyles, which those people indured at the Spaniardes handes, from the peere 1510. vntill this present. I will onely rehearse two or three actes, by the whiche it may bee iudged of the rest, innumerable and excessiue, and worthy all tormentes and fire.

In the Isle of the Trinitie, whiche is farre greater and more fertile then the Isle of Scicile, and ioyneth with the firme lande of the coaste of Paria, and where the people are the best disposed, and moste enclined to vertue in their kinde, of all

P the

the Indians, as they went, there a captaine Rouer in the yeere, 1510. accompanied with 60. or 70. other petie theeues well appointed: they published among the Indians by proclamations, and other publike sermons, that they should come and dwell and liue with them in that Ile. The Indians receiued them as their owne bowels and babes: and as well the Lordes as subiectes serued them with exceeding readines, bringing them to eate frō day to day, as much as might suffice to feede, as manie moe people. For this is the liberality of all these Indians of the new world, to bestow on the Spaniards of al that they haue in great abundance. The Spanish build a great house of timber, in the which the Indians should dwell all together: for the Spanishe would haue it so, that there should be one only house for all, and no more, to compasse that, which they had alredie premeditate to do, & did it. When they laid the thetch vpon the binding staues or sparres, and had alreadie couered to the height of two mens length, to the end that those that were within might not see those that were without, vnder colour to hasten forward the woorke, þ it might be the sooner dispatched, they set a great number of people within, the Spaniards deuiding themselues, the one part of them being bestowed without, compassing the house round about with their weapons, because of those that might get forth, the other part of them presse into the house: Thus laying hands on their swordes, they began to threaten the Indians naked as they were, to kill them if they did stirre, and then bound them. And those which fled they hewed them in peeces: Howbeit som of the Indies which fled, both of the hurt & not hurt, with others that had not come within the house, toke their bowes & arrowes and assembled themselues in another house, about an hundred or two hundred persons: And as they kept the gate, the Spaniard set fire on the house, & burned them aliue. After with their purchase, which might bee of an hundred or fourescore persons of them which they had bounde: they get them to the Ile of saint Iohn, where they solde the one moitie, and thence to the Ile of Hispaniola: where they solde the other moity. As I reprehended the captaine for this notable treason, at the same time, and at the same Ile of Saint Iohn, hee made an answere: Syr, quiet your
selfe.

selfe for that matter. So haue they commanded me to doe, and giuen me instruction which sent mee : that if I coulde not take them by warre, I shoulde take them vnder countenance and colour of peace. And in truth the Captaine tolde mee that in all his life, he neuer had founde father nor mother, but in this Isle of the Trinitie, in respect of the friendly courtesies the Indians had shewed him. And this hee spake to his owne greater confusion and aggrauating for the surcharge of his owne offences. They haue done other things semblable vnto these infinite, in this firme lande : apprehending the poore people contrary to the safe conduct promised. Let it now be weighed, what maner of doings these are, and whether the Indians in this wise taken, might iustly be made slaues.

At another time, the religious Fryars of saint Dominicks order, being determined to goe preache, and to conuert those nations , who had not the light of the doctrine for to saue their souls, as is the case at this day of the Indians : they sent a religious man licentiate in diuinitie, a man vertuous & holy, with a laie man of his order his companion, to the ende hee shoulde take a viewe of the Countrie, to trauerse acquaintance with that people, and search out a place commodious to builde monasteries. The religious being arriued : they receiued them as Angelles commen from heauen : and hearde with great affection, attention, and willingnesse such wordes as the religious at that time were able to giue them to vnderstand, more by signes then otherwise, for they knew not the tongue. It came to passe that there arriued there another ship, after that the ship in whiche the religious men came was departed thence, and the Spanish in this vessell, keeping their diuelish custome, by suttelty without the knowledge of the religious, carried away the Lord of the countrie called Alfonso: were it that Friars had giue him this name, or els others. For the Indians loue & desire to beare the name of the Christians, desiring incontinet that it may be giuen them euen before they know any thing, that they may be baptized.   They induced fraudilently this Don Alfonso to come aboord their ship with the lady his wife, & other persons, making semblance to go about to feast the. In the end there entred seuenteene persons, together with the

Lord

Lord and his Lady: the Lord trusting that the religious persons being entred into his Countrie , woulde keepe the Spaniardes from doyng any wrong: for otherwise hee woulde neuer haue put himselfe in the handes of the Spanish. The Indians therfore thus being in the ship, the traiterous Spaniards hoysed sayles, and away they went to Hispaniola with them, there selling them for slaues. All the Countrie seeing that their Lorde & soueraigne Lady were carried away, they run to the religious men, purposing to kill them. The poore men seeing so great a villany, were of themselues at a point to dye for sorrowe: and it is well to be beleeued of them, that they woulde rather haue gyuen their lyues in the quarrell, then to haue accorded that anye such iniury should haue been committed: specially considering that was euough to hinder the course begun, so as those poore Heathens should neuer, neither heare, nor hearing beleeue the worde of God. Howbeit, they appeased the Indians in the best maner they could, saying that they woulde write to them at Hispaniola by the first ship that went, & would take suche care and order in the matter, that their soueraigne should be restored them againe with those that were in his companie. God sent immediately vpon a ship thither, no doubt for the greater confirmation of the damnation of those which there gouerned, and they wrote to the Spanishe religious men that were in the Isle of Hispaniola. They cry out, and call heauen and earth to witnesse against them, both first, & sundrie times after: But the Iudges of the audience, would neuer giue them audience to do thē iustice, for because thēselues had part in the bootie of the Indiās, which the tyrants had so against all right & reason take, The two religiovs men, which had promised the Indians of the countrie, that their Lord Don Alfonso, with others shold come home with the rest within foure moneths, seeing ꝑ they came not neither in 4. nor 8. made thēselues redy to the death, & to giue their life, whiche they had gaged before they came out of Spaine, if neede shoulde bee, and in that sort the Indians tooke vengeance on thē in killing them iustly, notwithstanding that they were innocent: for because that they thought that the religious men had beene the occasion of this treason, and for because they sawe that, that whiche they had certified and promised them, tooke not effect: to witte, that within foure monethes they shoulde haue

home their Lorde: and for that, at that time they knewe not, and
nowe as yet they knowe not in that countrey, that there is any
difference betweene the religious well disposed: and the tyrants,
theeues, and robbers the Spaniardes.   Those religious men
therefore right happie, suffered vniustly , and for the wrong so
suffered, there is no doubt but they are very martyres , and doe
raigne at this day with God in the kingdome of heauen in blisse,
who woulde that by their obedience they shoulde be sent thither,
and should haue an entent, to preache and spredde the holy faith,
and saue all those soules, and suffer those afflictions , and death
it selfe when it shoulde be presented vnto them for Iesus Christe
his sake crucified.

An other time, by reason of the great tyrannies and execrable actes of the cursed ones, bearing the name of Christians, the
Indians slewe other two religious men of Saint Dominickes
order, and one of Saint Frauncis. Whereof I can be a good
witnesse for that I escaped at the time miraculously from the
same death, of the which it shoulde be a harde matter to entreat,
and woulde bee to amase men, by reason of the grieuousnes and
horiblenesse of the case. Wherefore I will not lay it abroad (for
being too tedious) vntill his tyme, and at the day of iudgement it
shall bee more euident , when God shall take vengeance of the
theeueries so horrible and so abhominable as are doone by those
which beare the name of Christians against the Indians.

An other tyme in those Prouinces at the Cape of the Co-
dera (as they call it) there was a towne, the Lorde whereof
was named Higueroto, a name eyther proper to the person,
or it may bee common to the Lordes of the place. This Lorde
was so bounteous, and his people so vertuous and seruiceable,
that as many Spaniardes as came thither by shippe, they founde
there good entertaynement, meate, lodging, all cheering, and
refreshing.   This saide Lorde had also deliuered many from
death of those which were fledde thither out of other Prouinces,
where they had ryoted, and tyrannised , and come thither sicke,
and halfe dead for hunger : whom they refreshed, and afterward
sent them away safe, to the Ile of Perles , where there were
Spaniardes , and might haue slayne them if hee had woulde,

with-

without that euer any shoulde haue knowen it. And shortely to say the Spanish did call the Subiectes of Higurroto, the house and harbour of euery bodie. A captiue tyraunt aduised him selfe to outrage that people also, when as they thought them selues sure enough: and getting him to a shippe, hee had there inuited a greate number of people to come a boorde her as they were accustomed to doe, and to trust the Spaniardes.

A great nūber of people being entred into her, men, women, and children, hee hoysed saples, and went to the Ile of Saint John, where hee soulde them all for slaues.

I came at the same instant to the Ile of Saint John, and I sawe the tyrant, and vnderstood what he had done. Hee had destroyed all that towneship: whereby he did great harme to all other his fellow tyrants, wonted to rob, and roue all along those coasts, insomuch as they had in abomination this act so hydeous, being bereft thereby of their harbour, and house of retire, as ordinarie & familiar vnto them as it had bin their own homes house.

I deport me to recount the mischieues infinite, and cases abominable, which haue bin vsed in that countrey, and are vsed as yet.

They haue singled out at times from all this coaste, the which was very wel peopled, vnto the Iles of S. John & Hispaniola, aboue two millions of soules, seased vpon by their purchases in thieuing and robbing: which also euery one of them they haue slaine not long after, by thrusting them into the minerals and other tormoyls, besides the great numbers there were there already before time, as we haue aboue said. And it is a pitifull thing, and able to make any heart to cleaue, were it neuer so harde, to see all this coast of a countrey most fertile, to bee lefte all naked and emptie of people.

It is a tried case, that they neuer conuey away their shippings of Indians so robbed & purchased, as I haue said, but that they cast the third part into the sea, besides those which they slay, whē they will sort thē to thēselues for their chafer. The cause is, that when as they will by all meanes atteine to the ende which they haue proposed to them selues: they haue need of a great number of people, for to draw a great deale of money, according to the

quantitie

quantitie of the slaues: & they prepare but a very small deale of sustenance and water, to serue but a few persons: to the ende that those tyrants whom they call purueyghours of the ships should not spend them much. And there is but euen scarse enough, saue to serue the Spaniardes turne which go a rouing and robbing: and there is alwayes wanting for the poore Indians. Wherefore also they die for hunger and thirst: and then there is none other remedie but to cast them ouer the boord into the sea. And verily a man among them did tell me, that from the Ile of Lucayos, where had been wrought great slaughters in this maner, vnto the Ile of Hispaniola, which are a threescore, or seuentie leages, there trended a ship all alongst, without that it had either compasse or mariners carde, being guided onely by the tracke of dead Indians carkasses, flotting vppon the seas, of them whiche had been cast in.

And after they be landed in the Ile, whither they bring them to make sale of them: it is to make an heart to pearue of whosoeuer, haue he neuer so litle compassion, to behold them naked and famished, fall downe and faint for hunger and thirst, women, and aged men, and children.

Afterwardes they soone after they separate them, as it were Lambes, the fathers from the children, and the wiues from the husbandes, in making troupes of them of tenne or twentie persons, and so cast lottes on them, to the ende, those cursed purueighours should take their share, which are those who do equipe or rig, and furnish two or three ships for the nauy of those tirants, pirates, and rouers, robbing by sea & land, sealing vpon all they come by, and pulling the poore men out of their owne housen. And looke when the lot falleth vppon the flock where there were amõg thẽ any old or sick persõ, y tyrant to whõ y same escheated, would say: That the diuell take the olde graybeard, why doest thou giue him mee, to the ende I shoulde goe burie him? And this sicke rascall, what haue I to doe that hee shoulde fall out to my lotte: to the ende, I shoulde bee his Phisition to cure him? Hereby a man may see, in what estimation the Spaniardes haue the Indians, and howe they accomplishe the commaundement of God, touching the loue of their neighbour, of the which

P 4   depen-

dependeth the lawe and the Prophetes. The tyrannie whiche the Spanishe exercise ouer the Indians , to fishe for Pearles, is one of the cruellest and cursedest thynges that is in the worlde.

There is no hell in this life, nor other desperate state in this worlde, that may be compared vnto it : although that the trade of golde finding, be in his kinde, very grieuous, and very miserable. They let them into the sea, three, or foure, or fiue, fadome forthdownright vnder water , from the morning vntyll sunnesette, where they are continually flitting without stint, to plucke oysters, in the which are engendred the pearles. They surge vp aboue the waters , with a nette full of oysters to take breath : where standeth readie a Spanishe tormentor, in a little cocke boate, or a brigantine, and if the poore wretches stay neuer so litle while, to rest them selues: they all to bee buffet them with their fistes, and draw them by the haire into the water to returne to their fishing. Their sustenaunce is fishe, and the same very fish which contayneth the pearles, and the bread Cacabi, or some Mahis, which are the kindes of bread of that countrey : the one of very slender nourishment, the other is not easie to bee made into breade, of the which also , they neuer giue them their belly full.

The beddes that they lodge them in a nights, is to set them by the heeles, their bodies requoyling on the coulde grounde, in a payre of stockes for feare of running away. Sometymes they are drowned in the sea , and at their fishing and trauaple of piking of pearles , and neuer rise vp agayne aboue the water : because the Bunches and Whirlepooles (they call them Tuberones and Maroxos) two kinde of monsters of the sea most cruell, which deuour a man all whole, and those doe kill them and eate them.

Let it nowe here be considered , whither in this purchase of Pearles, the commaundementes of God, touching the loue of God, and our neyghbours be kept, or not : when they throwe those people into daunger of bodyes and soules. For they slay their neigbours by their couetousnesse , without that they receiue , or fayth , or sacramentes , or els they prolonge
them

them in a state of life so horrible, that they bring them to their
ende, and consume them in a few dayes. For it is impossible, that
men should be able to liue any long seasō vnder the water without taking breath, the continuall cold percing them: & so they die
cōmōly, parbraking of blood at ÿ mouth: because of the kitting
together of their chestes, or bulke of the breast arising thereof,
that they are so continually without breathing vnder the water,
and of the blooddy fluxe, caused by the cold. Theyr haires, which
by nature are cole blacke, alter and become after a branded rus-
sette, like to the haires of the seawolues. The salt peeter breaketh
out of their shouldiers, in such sort, that they seeme to bee a kind
of monsters in the shape of men, or els some other kinde of men.
They dispatched in ridding about this insupportable trauayle, or
rather to speake rightly, this diuelish torment, all ÿ Lucayan Indians which were in the Iles, hauing sauoured this gaynes, and
euery Indian was woorth vnto them a fiftie, or an hundred
Castillans. They made an open marte of them, notwithstanding it were inhibited them, by the magistrate otherwise vnmer-
cifull: for the Lucayens were good swimmers. They also, a-
bout these thinges haue slayne a number of the people of other
prouinces.

Of the riuer Yuia Pari.

There runneth through the prouince of Paria, a riuer named Yuia Pari, more then two hundred leagues within
land from the head. There entred the same riuer, an vnluckie
tyraunt, a great manie leagues vpwarde, in the yeere, one
thousande, fiue hundred, twentie and niene with a foure hundred menne or more: whiche there wroght greate slaughters,
burning aliue, and putting to the edge of the swoorde, an infinite sorte of Indians, whiche were in their landes and housen
doing hurt to no creature, and therefore secure, and mistrusting
nothing.

In the ende hee dyed an euill death, and his Nauie was
disperaged: albeit that other tyraunts there were which succeeded

ded him in his mischieuousnesses and tyrannies : and yet at this day thither they goe, destroying, and slaying, and plunging into hell the soules for whom the sonne of God shed his blood.

Of the realme of Venesuela.

THe yeere 1526. the king our Soueraigne, being induced by sinister informations and perswasions dammageable to the state, as the Spaniardes haue alwayes payned them selues to conceale from his Maiestie the dammages and dishonours which G O D and the soules of men, and his state doeth receiue in the Indies : graunted and committed a great realme, greater then all Spayne, that Uenesuela, with the gouernement and entier iurisdiction, vnto certayne Dutch Marchaunts, with certayne capitulations and conuentions accorded beetweene them.

These same entring the countrey with three hundred men: they found the people very amiable, & meeke as lambes, as they are all in those parties of the Indies, vntill the Spanish do outrage them. These set vpon them without comparison a great deale more cruelly, then any of the other tyrauntes, of the whiche wee haue spoken before : shewing them selues more vnnaturall and fierce, then raging tygars, or wolues, or ramping Lions. For they had the iurisdiction of the whole countrey, possessing it with more freedom, and vsing it with a greater care, and starker blinde madnes of couetyse, seruing their owne turnes with all practises and cheuisaunces, to get and gather golde and siluer, more then all they of whom hath bin spoken heretofore: hauing wholly shaken off all feare of God, and of the king: yea, hauing forgotten themselues to bee men.

These diuels incarnate haue laide desolate and destroyed, more then foure hundred leagues of most fertill lande, and therein, of prouinces exceeding and wonderfull, fayre vayles, to the breadth of fourtie leagues, and bournes verye great, full of

pea-people, and of golde. They haue slayne, and wholly discomfited great and diuers nations, so farre foorth as to abolishe the languages wonted to bee spoken, not leauing aliue that could skill of them: vnlesse some one or other, who had hid them selues in the caues and bowels of the earth, flying the dint of the sworde, so raging and plaging. They haue slayne, destroyed, and sent to hell by diuers and strange maners of cruelties and vngodlynesses, moe (J supposse) then foure or fiue millions of soules: and yet at this present, they cease not to doe the same, by infinite outrages, spoyles, add slaughters, which they haue committed, and doe commit dayly vnto this present. J will onely touch three or foure, by the which it may bee iudged of others, which they vsed to accomplish their destructions, and disolations aboue mentioned.

They tooke the Lord soueraigne of all the prouince without all cause, onely to bereeue him of his golde, giuing him also the torture: which Lorde vnbounde himselfe, and escaped from them into the mountaynes, wherefore also the subiectes rose and were in a mutinie, hiding the selues vpon the mountaynes, amongst the hedges and bushes. The Spaniardes make after to chase them, and hauing founde them, commit cruell massacres, and as many as they take aliue, they sell them in port sale for slaues.

In diuers prouinces, yea in all where they became before that they tooke the Soueraigne Lorde, the Indies went to receyue them with songes, and daunces, and with presents of gold in great quantitie.

The payment made them, was, to bee put to the edge of the sworde, and hewen in peeces. One time, as they went to receyue the Spanishe in the fashion abouesayde: the Dutche Captayne tyraunt, caused to bee put in a thatched house a greate number of people, and hackled in peeces.

And beeing on high, neere the top of the house certayne beames which diuers had got vpon, auoyding the bloodoy handes and swordes of those people (O mercilesse beastes) the diuelishe man, sent to put to fire, wherby as many as there were, were burned aliue. By this meanes the countrey remained very desert, ç people flying into the mountaines, where they hoped to saue theselues.

They

They came into another great prouince, in the confines of the prouince and realme or Saint Martha, where they found the Indians peaceable in their boroghs, & in their house, doing their busines: they continued a long time with them, eating their store, and the Indians serued them, as if they had to receiue of them their life and safegarde, supporting their continuall oppressions, and vsuall outragiousnesses, which are intollerable: besides that one Spanishe glutton, eateth more in one day, then woalde suffice an whole housholde of more then ten Indians. They gaue them at that time, a great quantitie of golde, of their owne good will, ouer & besides, other seruices innumerable, which they did vnto them. At the ende as these tyrants would depart the place, they aduised to pay them for their lodging, in this manner.

The Almain tyrant gouernour, commaunded to take suche Indians as they could, with their wiues and children, and that they should shut them vp within an inclosure, wounded in of purpose, letting them know, that who so would come forth, and bee let go free, that he should redeeme himselfe at the pleasure of the vniust gouernour: in giuing so much golde for himselfe, so much for his wife, and so much for euery polle of his children. And yet to presse them the more, he commanded to giue them nothing to eate, vntill such time as they had perfourmed the quantity of gold inflicted them for their raunsome. Many sent to their housen for golde, and bought out themselues as they were able, and those same were deliuered, and went abroad about their busines to get their liuing. The tyrant sent certain Spanish thieues & robbers, to go take them againe the second time, after they had bin redeemed. They are carried to the perclose, and there wrung with hunger and thirst, to the ende, that they shoulde yet once agayn pay for their freedom. And there were many amongst them, which were taken and ransommed two or three sundry times. Others which had not to giue, for because they had all they had, he let them within the toyle dye for hunger.

And in this maner hath bin destroyed a prouince very riche of people and golde, the which hath a vale or bourne of fourtie leagues, where hath beene brent a borough of the receite of a thousande housholdes.

This

This Tyrant resolued with himselfe to pearce farther into the countrie, with a great desire to discouer on that side, þ same hill of Peru. By occasion of which accursed voyage both hee and others carried foorth with them, Indians infinite, loden with two or three quintalles weight, and beeing enchained. If any were weake or wearie, fainting for hunger, or trauelling, they cut incontinent his head off euen with the coller of the chaine that yoked them: because they shoulde not neede to vnhamper the others that went with the same collers aboute their neckes, and so tombled the head on the one side, and the bodie on the other. And the load of him that had so failed was distributed and bestowed vpon others. To tel of the Prouinces, whiche hee hath layed desart, and the townes and places which hee hath brent, for all the houses are thetched, and to number the nations which hee hath slaine, and the crueltie, and murders particuler, which hee hath committed by the way, it would be a thing scarce credible: howbeit very true and wonderfull. In this same very course and steppes marched sithence the other tyrants, who came from the said Uenesuela, and others of the Prouince of S. Martha, with the selfe same holy intention to discouer the same sacred golden palace of Peru: and founde the whole countrie in length more then two hundred leagues so burned, dispeopled, & spoyled, hauing been before most notablie peopled and most fertill, as hath been said, that themselues as very tyrantes and sauage beastes as they were, wondered and stood astonished to see the trackes of the destructions so lamentable, wheresoeuer he had passed.

All these thinges haue been giuen in euidence with the depositions of many witnesses by the Atturney of the councel of the Indies, and the euidences are kept amongst the Recordes of the same councell: and yet haue they neuer burnt aliue, any of those execrable tyrants. And this is nothing of all that whiche hath beene proued, of the great outrages and mischieues which these haue committed. For as much as the ministers of iustice, which vntill this time haue bin in the Indies, by reason of their great wilfull and damnable blyndnesse, haue neuer troubled themselues to examine the offences, spoyles, and murders, which

J.3

haue

haue beene wrought, and yet presently are wrought by the tyrants in the Indies : saue only they will say, because suche hath
cruelly intreated the Indies, the king hath lost of his reuenews
so many thousande Castilians in rent, and this little verdict o-
uer general and confused, must suffice for the disclaime of so many villanies. And yet that litle which they take vpon them, they
doe not auerr, nor deliuer vpon, as they ought to do. For if they
had regarde of their dutie to God and the king, it woulde bee
founde, that those Almaine tyrants haue robbed the king of a-
boue three thousand Castillans of gold. For those prouinces of
Uenesuela with the others which they haue laid waste, and dispeopled more then four hundred leagues forthright, as hath bin
saide, is a region the most blisfull, and the richest of golde, and
was the best peopled of any in the worlde : in such sort, that they
haue disturned from the kinges cofers, and occasioned the losse
in this Realm of aboue two millions of rent, within seuenteene
yeeres sithence by past, that these enemies of God and the king
haue begunne to destroy it: neither is there any hope that euer
those losses will be repayred as long as the worlde shall indure:
vnlesse it be, that God shold myraculously rayse as many millions of soules as are deceased. It shall not bee out of the way to
consider, of what sortes and howe excessiue haue beene the damages, dishonours, blasphemies, & infamies, which God & his
lawe hath receiued: And wherewithall may bee recouered &
recompensed the losse of so many soules as burne in hell fire
through the auarice and crueltie of those tyrants Almains, shall
I say, or All-uains?

Onely I will conclude the discourse of their vngraciousnesse and crueltie heerewith. That is, that sithence they entred
the country vnto this present, that is to say, these seuenteene yeres
they haue sent by Sea a great number of ships loaden & stuffed
with Indians, to make sale of them as slaues at S. Martha, at
the Isles of Hispaniola, and of Iamayca, and at Saint Johns
Isle, moe then one million : and doe sende dayly, as nowe this
yeere one thousand, fiue hundred, fortie two : the Court of the
Audience royall notwithstanding stablished, for, and at Hispaniola, right well seeing all this, and dissimuling to see it, yea, fa-
uouring

uouring and supporting all the matter : as likewise they haue had theyꝛ eyes bended at all the other tyꝛannies and ranſackings infinite, which hath been done in all this coaſt of this firme land which are about foure hundꝛed leagues, the which haue been and nowe are vnder their iuriſdiction, like vnto Ueneſuela, ꝭ ſaint Martha : all which the ſaid court might very well haue empea-ched and remedied.   There is none other cauſe of putting all theſe Indians vnder yoke of bondage, ſaue the only peruerſe, wilfully blinde, and obſtinate greedines, and inſatiable wꝛet-chedneſſe of theſe moſt couetous tyꝛants, and all to haue, and heape vp goods like as hath had all the reſt thꝛoughout all the Indies, ramping theſe ſilly lambes and ſheepe out of their hou-ſes, and carrying their wiues and childꝛen in the maners of pꝛo-ceeding ſo cruel and execrable as hath been ſaid, bꝛanding them with the kings marke, to make them vendible foꝛ ſlaues.

Of the Prouinces of the firme lande, or quarter that is called Florida.

INto theſe Pꝛouinces went thꝛee tyꝛantes at thꝛee diuers times ſince the peere 1510, oꝛ 1511. there to put in vꝛe the actes which others, and two of them from among themſelues haue committed in other quarters of the Indians : to the end to aſpyꝛe to high degrees, in no reſpect conuenient to their per-ſons, bigher then their merites in the cōmon wealth could con-ceaue, with the blood ꝭ deſtruction of their neighbours : and they are dead all thꝛee of an euill death, ꝭ their houſes likewiſe haue been deſtroyed with them, the which they had builded in times paſt, with the blood of mankinde, as I can be a ſufficient witnes of all thꝛee, and their memoꝛie is nowe aboliſhed from of the face of the earth, as if they had neuer beene in this woꝛlde. They left all this Countrie in diſoꝛder, and confuſion , and their owne manners in infamie and hoꝛꝛoꝛ, foꝛ certaine ſlaugh-ters whiche they did there , notwithſtanding not ſo manie,

foꝛ

for as much as God plagued them with death before they coulde doe any more, and kept them from this outrage in this place, for the euils that I knowe, and haue seene that they did in other partes of the Indies.

The fourth tyrant, that came last in the yere. 1538. cunningly aduised, and beeing fully furnished : it is three yeeres since there is no tidinges concerning him. Wee are certaine that incontinent after his entrie thither : hee hath behaued himself cruelly, and since hath beene as a man vanished, That if he be aliue, hee and his mainies haue destroyed these three yeeres a great many mightie peoples, if hee hath found any in his enquest as hee hath gone : for sure he is one of the notoriousest and best experimented amongest them that haue done the most hurts, mischieues, and destructions in many Realmes with their consorts : wherefore I beleeue that God hath giuen him like end vnto the others.

Three or foure yeeres after the writing of the aboue written, came out of the Florida the head of the petie tyrants which went thither with this captaine tyrant, that there left his bones : of whome wee vnderstood the cruelties and euilles, whiche there during his life time principailly, and vnder his conduct & gouernment, and since after his cursed death, the vnnaturall men haue executed against the Indians innocent, and harmeful to none, to verifie that which I had prognosticate before, they being so excessiue, that they haue the more confirmed the rule by mee set downe before at the beginning, that the farther they proceeded to discouer, destroy, and to waste countries and lands : the more cruelties and notorious wickednesses they woulde doe against God, and against their neighbours. It loatheth mee to recount those actes so cursed, ghastly, and bloodie, not of men but of sauage beastes : and therfore I would not trouble my head to stand rehearsing those which followed afterwards.

They found many great nations, and wise common weales well instituted for pollicie and ordinances. They executed vpon them great slaughters after their custome, to the ende to imprint in their heartes an awe. They martyred and murdered them, and loded them with weightie packes like beastes. And when

and

any was foreweeried or forespent, to the ende they shoulde not
need to loose the chain, in the which they were giuen in collers,
before they come at him that fainted, they pare off the head from
the collar bymme, the Troncke tombling one way, and the
chaine another: as we haue before recounted to haue beene vsed
otherwise.

Entring a borough, where they were receaued with ioy, and
the Indians giuing them to eate their fill, and giuing them of
Indians more then sixe hundred to carry their fardels, carrying
the heaste of beastes in their seruice, and dressing their horses: the
tyrants being departed thence, a captaine kinsman of the principall tyrant returned to rob the people, being without distrust &
without feare, and slue with the thrustes of Launce the Lorde
and Kyng of the Countrie, executing besides other cruelties.

In another borough, forasmuch as it seemed them that they
were a little too neere neighbours, & stood more on their warde,
for the actes villanous and infamous, which they had hearde
of them: they put to the edge of the sworde and launce, young &
olde, great and little, subiect and soueraigne, taking to mercy no
creature whosoeuer.

The head tyrant caused to pare off the nose and lips downe
to the chin of a great number of Indians, yea, more then 200.
(as is said) that they had caused to bee sent for from a certaine borough, or it may bee came of their owne good will. And
thus in this estate so rufull, and in these sorrowes and anguishes of blood streaming downe, they sent them away: to the end
they might go carry newes of the holy woorkes and myracles,
which these preachers of the sacred catholike faith, & baptised,
had wrought.

Let it nowe bee iudged, what kinde of people these were,
what loue they beare to the Christians, and howe they doe beleeue that God is, whome they say to bee perfectly mercifull
and righteous, and that the lawe and the religion, of the
whiche they make profession, and doe vaunt themselues, is
without blemish. The mischiefes are exceeding sore & strange,

K   which

which those vngracious captiues, children of perdition there committed. And thus the desperate and vnluckie Captayne dyed without confession : and we neede not to doubte but that he lyeth buried in hell : if algates God of his infinite mercy secretly dispensed in his hidden wisdome hath not preuented him, not dealing with him, after his demerites, in respect of his vngracious lewdnes.

Of the riuer of la Plata, that is
to say, of siluer.

Sthence the yeere, one thousande fiue hundred, and two or three and twentie : certaine Captaines made three or foure voyages vppe the Riuer of Plata, where there are great Prouinces and Realmes, and nations well ordered and endued with vnderstanding. In generall we vnderstood, that they haue made there greate butcheries and inuasions : but like as this Countrie is farre discoasted from the Indies most famous, so we are not able, to quote the notablest points in particuler. Wee doubt no whit notwithstanding, but that they haue done and doe keepe as yet at this houre the same order of proceedings as hath beene kept, and are in other quarters : for they bee the selfesame Spaniardes, and there are amongest them of those same, whiche haue trauersed in other actes and exploites such as hath beene specified. Moreouer, theyr going thither, is to beecome riche and great Lordes as well as others : that which cannot bee done without spoyling, robbinge, slaying, and extirping the Indians, in maner and order holden by the others.

After the writing the abouesaid, I haue vnderstood, that of a truth, they haue wasted and dispeopled great Prouinces and Realmes in that Countrie, exercising strange slaughters & cruelties vpon these poore people there, for the whiche they haue abled themselues as forwarde in wickednesse, or forwarder then
any

any other, as hauing the commoditie by the greater distance frō Spaine, to sinne the Freer, and by occasion therof haue liued the more disordered and farthest off from iustice : howbeit that in all the Indies, there hath beene no regarde of Iustice, as appeareth sufficiently, by that which hath beene aboue saide.

Amongest an infinite sort of other thinges wee reade at the counsell table for the Indies, these also which shall bee spoken of hereafter. A tyrant gouernour gaue in commande to certaine his bands to goe assault the Indians, and that if they gaue them not to eate they shoulde kill them al. They went armed to this authoritie, And for because the Indians would giue thē none as being open enemies , more for feare of the sighte of them, as flying from them then for want of liberalitie, they put to the edge of the swoorde more then fiue thousande soules.

Item a certaine number of the folke of the Countrie came to put themselues into their handes, and presented them their seruice, whome at aduenture they had sent for : and for because they came not so soone, or for because they woulde after their accustomed fashion, engraue in them an horrible and astonishable terrour : the gouernour commaunded that they should put them into the handes of other Indians, whome they holde for their enemies : whereupon they came weeping and crying, and beseeching them that they woulde slay them, themselues, and not deliuer them into the power of their enemies, and hauing no mind to yeede out of their houses where they were, they were cut in peeces, crying, and saying : Wee come to serue you in peace, and do you slay vs ? Our bloud remaine imprinted on this wall, for a witnesse against you of our vniust death, and your barbarous crueltie. Certes, this was an act of speciall marke, worthie to be remembred, and much more to bee lamented.

K 2.   Of

Of the mightie Realmes, and large
Prouinces of Peru.

IN the yeere 1531. went another great tyrant with certaine other consortes, to the Realmes of Peru, where entring with the same title and intention, and with the same proceedings as all the rest before gone, forasmuch as hee was one of them, which had of long time beene exercised in all kindes of crueltties and murders, which had beene wrought in the firme lande sithence the yeere one thousande fiue hundred, and ten, hee tooke encouragement to accrewe in crueltics, murders, & robberies: beeing a man without loyaltie and truth, laying waste Cities and Countries, bringing them to nought, and vtterly vndoeyng them by slaying the inhabitaunts, and beeing the cause of all the euils, whiche ensued in that Countrie : that I am right well assured, that there is not a man that can recounte them and represent them to the eyes of the Readers, as is requisite, vntill such time that wee shall see them and knowe them at the day of iudgement. Astouching my self, if I woulde take vppon mee, to recounte the deformitie, qualitie and circumstances of some one, I were not able to decipher them, acording to that which is conuenient.

Hee slue and laide waste at his firste arriuall with a mischiefe certaine boroughes, from whome hee pillaged a greate quantitie of Golde. In an Ilande neere to the same prouinces, named Pagna, well peopled and pleasant, the Lord thereof with his people receiued them as it had been Angels from heauen : and sixe monethes after, when as the Spanishe had eaten vppe all their prouision : They discouered also vnto them the corne whiche they kept vnder grounde, for them selues, their wiues, and their childrẽ, against a drie time and barren, : making them offer of all, with teers plentiful, to spende and eate at their pleasure. The recompenee in the ende whiche they made them, was, to put to the edge of the sworde and launce, a great quantitie of those people. And those
whom

whom they could take aliue, they made them slaues: with other
cruelties great and notable which they committed, dispeopling
as it were all that Ile.

From thence they make to the prouince of Tumbala, whiche
is in the firme lande, where they slay and destroy as many as
they coulde come by. And because all the people were fled as
affrighted by their horrible actes, they sayde that they made an
insurrection, and rebelled against the king of Spayne. This
tyraunt had this policie, and kept this order of proceeding, that,
vnto all those whom hee tooke, or vnto others which presented
him with golde or siluer, or other thinges which they had : hee
commaunded them to bring more, vntill such time as hee perceiued that either they had no more, or that they brought him no
more. And then hee woulde say, that hee accepted them for the
vassals and lieges of the kinge of Spaine, and made muche of
them: and woulde cause it to bee proclaymed at sounde of two
trompettes, that from thence forth they woulde take them no
more, and that they woulde doe them no maner harme at all :
setting it downe for good and lawfull, all that whatsoeuer hee
had robbed from them.

And that hee put them in feare with newes so abhominable
which hee spredde amongst them, before hee receiued them into
the safegarde and protection of the king, as though that after
they were receiued vnder the protection of the king, they woulde
not oppresse them, robbe them, lay them waste and desolate any
more, yea and as though he had not destroyed them.

A fewe dayes after, the king & Emperour of those realmes,
named Atabaliba, came accompanied with a number of naked people, bearing their ridiculous armour, not knowing neyther howe swordes did carue, nor speares did pearce, nor horses
did runne, nor who or what were the Spaniardes : who if the
diuelles had any money, woulde set them selues in enquest to
goe robbe them. Hee commeth to the place where they were,
saying : Where are these Spaniardes? Let them come, I will
not stirre a foote, till they satisfie mee for my subiectes whome
they haue slayne, and my boroughs which they haue dispeopled,
and for my wealth, which they haue bereeued mee.

The

The Spaniardes set against him, and slue and infinite forte of his people : they tooke him also in person, who came caried in a litter born vpon mens shouldiers. They treat with him, to the ende that hee shoulde raunsome himselfe. The king offereth to perfourme foure millions of Castillans, and performeth fifteene, they promise to release him : notwithstanding in the ende, keeping nor faith nor trueth (as they neuer kept any in the Indies, vnto the Indians) they layed vnto his charge altogether vntruly, that by his commaundement the people assembled.

The king answered, that in all the countrey there mooued not a leafe of a tree, without his good will : that if there assembled any people, they were to beleeue that it was by his commaundement, and as touching himselfe that hee was prisoner, and they might slay him.

All this notwithstanding, they condemned him to bee brent aliue: but at the request of some certayne, the Captayne caused him to bee strangled : and beeing strangled, hee was burned.

This king vnderstanding his sentence, sayde: Wherefore will you burne mee ? What trespasse haue I done yee ? Did not you promise mee to set mee at libertie, if I gaue you the golde ? and haue I not performed more then I promised? Seeinges you will needes haue it, so ? sende mee to your king of Spayne: speaking other thinges, to the great confusion and detestation of the great wrongfulnesse that the Spaniardes vsed, whom in the ende they burned. Here let be considered the right and title of this warfare, the imprisonment of this prince, the sentence, and the execution of his death, and the conscience, whereby they possesse great treasures, as in deed they haue robbed in those realmes from this king and other seuerall lordes infinite.

As touching the innumerable cruelties, and notable, for y mischiefes and enormities withall committed in the rooting out of those peoples by them, who call themselues Christians: I will here rehearse some certayne, the which a fryer of S. Frauncis order sawe at the beginning, and the same certified vnder his name and signe : sending them into all those quarters, and amongst others into this realme of Castile, whereof I retayne a copie in my keeping in the which it is thus written:

I

I Frier Marke, of the order of Saint Frauncis, commissarie ouer the other friers of the same order in the prouinces of Peru, and who was one of the first religious men, w entred into the saide prouinces with the Spaniardes : doe say, bearing true testimonie of certayne things, the which I haue seene with mine eyes in that countrey , namely, concerning the entreating and conquestes made ouer the naturall inhabitauntes of the countrey: first of all, I am an eyed witnesse, and haue certayn knoweledge, that those Indians of Peru, are a people the most kinde hearted that hath been seen among all the Indians, beeing curteous in conuersation, and friendly vnto the Spaniardes.

And I sawe them giue to the Spanishe in abundaunce, golde, siluer , and precious stones, and all that was asked them, and that they had, doing them all kinde of seruice lawfull. And the Indians neuer yee ded foorth to warre , but kept them in peace so long time, as they gaue them not occasion, by their euill entreating of them and their cruelties, but contrariwise receiued them with all amitie and honour in their boroughes, in giuing them to eate, and as many slaues mankinde and women kind, as they demaunded for their seruice.

Item I am witnesse, that without that the Indians gaue occasion : the Spanish as soone as they were entred the lande, after that the greate Cacike Atabaliba, had giuen to the Spanish more then two millions of gold, and had put into their power the whole countrie without resistance, incontinent they burned the said Atabaliba which was Lord of the whole countrie.

And after him they brent his captayne generall Cochilimara, who had come to the gouernour in peace with other Lords. In the like maner also a fewe dayes after they burned a great Lorde named Chamba, of the prouince of Quito, without any fault at all , and without hauing giuen the least occasion that might bee.

In like maner they burned vniustly Schappera Lorde of the Canaries. Also they brent the feete of Aluis a great Lorde amongst all those which were in Quito , and caused him to endure sundrie other torments , to make him tell where was the gold of Atabaliba ; of the whiche treasure as it appeared , hee knewe nothing.
K 4

Also they brent in Quito Cosopanga, whc was gouernour of all the prouinces of Quito, which vpon the request to him first made by Sebastian of Bernalcasar Captayne vnder the gouernour, was come to them in peace : and onely because hee gaue them not golde so much as hee demaunded of him, they burned him with very many other Caciks and principall Lords. And for ought that I can vnderstand, the intente of the Spaniards was, that there shoulde not bee lefte aliue one Lorde in tho whole countrey.

Item I certifie, that the Spaniardes caused to assemble a great number of the Indians, and locked them vp in three great housen, as many as coulde be pozed in, and setting to fire, they burned them all, without that they had done the least thing that might bee, oz had giuen to the Spanishe the least occasion thereof whatsoeuer. And it came to passe, that a priest, who is named Ocanna, drewe a young boy out of the fire, in the which hee burned, which perceiuing an other Spaniarde tooke from out of his handes the boy, and flange him into the middest of the flames, where he was resolued into ashes together with others. The which Spaniarde returning the same day to the campe, fell downe dead suddenly, and mine aduice was hee should not bee buried.

Item I affirme, to haue seene with myne owne eyes, that the Spanishe haue cutte the handes, the noses, and the eares of the Indians, and of their women, without any other cause oz purpose, saue onely that so it came into their fantasie, and that in so many places and quarters, that it shoulde bee too tedious to rehearse. And I haue seene, that the Spanishe haue made their Mastiues runne vpon the Indians to rent them in pieces. And moreouer, I haue seene by them brent so many houses, and whole boroughes, oz towneshippes, that I am not able to tell the number. Also it is true, that they violently plucked the little infants from the mothers dugges, and taking them by the armes, did throwe them from them as farre as they coulde : Together with other enozmities and cruelties without any cause, whiche gaue me astonishment to behold them, and woulde be to long to rehearse them.

Item,

Item, I sawe when as they sent for the Cacikes and other principall Indians, to come see them in peace, and assuraunce to them made, promising them safe conduct: and incontinent as they were arriued, they burned them. They burned two whiles I was present, the one in Andon, and the other in Tumbala: and I coulde neuer preuaile with them to haue them deliuered from burning, preached I vnto them neuer so muche. And in God and my conscience, for ought that euer I coulde perceiue, the Indians of Peru, neuer lift themselues vp, nor neuer rebelled for any other cause, but for the euill entreating of the other side, as is manifest vnto euery one, and for iust cause: the Spaniardes destroying them tyrannously against all reason and iustice, with al their countrey, working vpon them so many outrages, that they were determined to die, rather then to suffer much an other time.

Item I say, that by the reporte of the Indians themselues, there is yet more golde hidden then is come to light, the whiche because of the vniustices and cruelties of the Spaniardes, they woulde not discouer, neyther euer will discouer, so long as they shall bee so euyll entreated, but will chuse rather to die with their fellowes.

Wherein GOD our Lorde hath been highly trespassed agaynst, and the kinges Maiestie euill serued, hauing beene defrauded in that, that his highnesse hath loste suche a countrey, as hath been able to yeelde sustenaunce to all Castile: for the recouerie of which countrey, it will be a matter of great difficulty, dispence, and charges.

All these hitherto are the formall woordes of the sayde religious person: the which are also ratified by the Byshoppe of Mexico, which witnesseth that the reuerende father hath to his knowledge affirmed all the aboue saide.

It is heere to bee considered, that the good father sayeth, that he sawe those thynges. For that, that bee hath beene fiftie, or an hundred leagues vp into the countrey, for the space of niene or tenne yeeres, and that at the very beginning, when there were not as yet but very fewe of the Spaniardes: but at

L

the

the ringing of the golde, there were quickly gathered and flocked thither foure o2 fiue thousande, which shedde them selues foo2th ouer many great realmes and p2ounces, mo2e then fiue hund2ed o2 sixe hund2ed leagues, the whiche countrey hath beene th2oughly dest2oyed, they executing still the selfe same p2actises, and others mo2e barbarous and cruell.

Of a veritie from that day vnto this p2esente, there hath beene dest2oyed and b2ought to desolation moe soules then hee hath coumpted: and they haue with lesse reuerence of GOD o2 the King, and with lesse pittie then befo2e, abolished a great part of the linage of mankinde.

They haue slayne vnto this day in these same realmes (and yet dayly they doe slay them) moe then foure millions of soules.

Certayne dayes passed, they p2icked in shooting with dartes of reedes to death a mightie Queene, wife of Eling, who is yet king of that Realme, whom the Spaniardes by laying handes vpon him compelled to rebell, and in rebellion hee persisteth.

They tooke the Queene his wife, and so as hath beene sayde, slue her against all reason and iustice, beeing greate with childe as shee was, as it was said onely to vexe her husband withall.

If it shoulde bee expedient to recounte the particularities of the cruelties and slaughters that the Spanishe haue committed, and yet dayly doe committe in Peru: without all doube they shoulde bee so frightfull, and in so great number, that all that wee haue hitherto saide of the other partes of the Indies, woulde bee shadowed, and it woulde seeme a small matter in the respecte of the grieuousnesse and greate number hereof.

Of

Of the newe realme of
Grenado.

WIthin the yeere 1539. there tooke their flight together sundzy tyzantes, flocking from Uenesuela, from
Saint Martha, and from Carthagene, to search foz the Perous:
and there were also others which came downe from Peru it
selfe to assay, to make a glade farther into the countrey: And they
found from beyond S. Marthas and Carthagene, 300. leagues
vp into the countrey, fertile landes, and admirable pzouinces,
full of infinite people, kinde hearted like the rest, and verye
riche, as well of golde as of pzecious stones, which they call emeraldes.

Unto the whiche Pzouinces they gaue the name of Newe
Grenado : Foz because that the tyzaunt whiche came first into
this countrey, was a grenado, boꝛne in our countrey. And
foz because that diuers wicked men and cruell of those whiche
roaued ouer this parte, were notozious butchers, making it an
occupation to shedde mans blood, hauing the pꝛactise and experience of the great fellonies afoze mentioned in moste part of
the other regions of the Indies : it is the cause why their diuelishe woozkes haue beene suche, and in so great number, whiche
the circumstaunces doe make appeare so monstrous and odious, that they haue farre exceeded the others, yea all the gifts
that haue gone befoze, done by others, oz by themselues in other
Pzouinces.

I will recounte some one oz other of an infinite whereof
they are guiltie, as doone by them within these thzee yeeres,
and whiche yet they cease not to committe. That is, that
a Gouernour, foz as muche as hee whiche robbed and slewe
in the newe Realme of Grenado, woulde not admitte him
foz consozte with him to robbe and sley as did hee : hee
pꝛocured an enquirie, and thereby euidence came in agaynst
him

him with sundrie witnesses, vpon the fact of his slaughters, disorders, and murders which hee had done, and doeth as yet vnto this day, the processe of which enquirie, together with the euidences was read, and is kept in the recordes of the counsell of the Indies.

The witnesses doe depose in the same enquirie, that the saide whole realme was in peace, the Indians seruing the Spaniards, giuing them to eate of their laboure, and labouring continually, and manuring the grounde, and bringing them muche golde and precious stones, suche as are emeraldes, and all that which they coulde and had: the townes, and the Lordeshippes, and the people being distributed amongst the Spaniardes euery one his share: which is all that they studie for, for that, that it is their meaneway to attayne to their last end and scope, to witte golde.

And all beeing subdued to their tyrannie and accustomed bondage, the tyrant the principall Captayne which commaunded ouer that countrey, tooke the Lorde and King of the countrey, and detayned him prisoner sixe or seuen monethes, exacting of him golde and emeraldes without cause or reason at all. The sayde king, who was named Bogata, for feare which they put him in, sayde that he woulde giue them an house full of golde: hoping that hee shoulde escape out of the handes of him whiche tormented him. And hee sent Indians which shoulde bringe him golde; and by times one after another, they brought in a great quantitie of golde and precious stones. But because the king did not giue an whole house full of golde, the Spaniardes his kill him: sithence that hee did not accomplishe that which he had promised.

The tyraunt commaunding that this king shoulde bee arraigned before him selfe: They common and accuse in this order the greatest king of all that countrey, and the tyraunt giueth sentence, condemning him to bee racked and tormented, if hee doe not furnishe forth the house full of golde.

They giue him the torture and the strapado with cordes: they flinge burnyng setyer vppon his naked belly: they lap

on

on boltes vpon his feete,which were fastened to one stake, and
gyrd his neck fast vnto another stake,two men holding both his
handes,and so they set fire vnto his feete : and the tyrant, comming vp and downe,nowe and then, willeth him to haue his
death giuen him by little and little, if hee made not readie the
golde. Thus they dispatched and did to death that noble Lord
in those torments, during the execution whereof, God manife-
sted by a signe,that those cruelties displeased him,in consuming
with fire all the towne where they were committed. All the
Spaniardes to the ende to followe their good Captaine,and hauing none other thing to doe,but to hackle in peeces those poore
innocents doe the like,tormenting with diuers and sauage torments euery Indian,both Cacike or Lorde of euery people or
peoples,with all their flocks,that were committed to their charges : those said Lordes with all their subiects seruing them,and
giuing them golde and emerauds as many as they coulde, and
as muche as they had : Tormenting them onely to the ende
they shoulde giue them more golde, and rich myner alles:thus
they bropled and dispatched all the Lordes of that Countrie.

For the great feare of the notorious cruelties,that one of the
petie tyrants did vnto the Indians, there transported himselfe
vnto the mountaines,in flying so great crueltie, a great Lorde
named Daytama, with many of his people. For this they
holde for their last remedie and refuge, if it might haue preuailed them ought : and this the Spaniardes call insurrection and
rebellion. Which the Captaine head tyrant hauing knowledge
of,he sendeth supplie of souldiers vnto the said cruel man : (for
whose cruelties sake, the Indians that were peaceable,and had
endured great tyrannies and mischiefes, were nowe gone into
the mountaines:)to the ende hee should pursue them.Who, because it sufficed not to bide them in the entrals of the earth, finding there a great multitude of people, slue and dispatched the,
aboue 500.soules,what men, what women,for they receiued none
to mercy. Also the witnesses depose,that the said Lord Daytama,before that the Spaniards put him to death,came to the cruell man,and brought him foure or fiue thousand Castillans, the
which notwithstanding he was murdred as is abouesaide.

An

Another time manie Indians beeing come to serue the Spaniardes, and seruing them with such humilitie and simplicitie, as they are accustomed to doe, reputing themselues assured: behold, the captaine of the towne where they serued, who commeth by night commaunding that those Indians should be put to the edge of the swordze, when they had supped, and whiles that they were a sleepe, taking their rest after the toyle which they sustained the day time. And this hee did, for that it seemed him necessary to do this massacre, to the end to engraue an awe of himself in the heartes of all the peoples of that countrie.

Another time the captaine commaunded to take an othe of the Spaniardes, to wit, howe many euery one had in his seruice of the Caciks, and principall Lordes, and Indias of the meaner sort: that incontinent they shoulde bee brought to the moste open place of the citie, where he commaunded that they shoulde be beheaded: thus were there at that time put to death a foure or fiue hundzed soules.

Moreouer these witnesses depose concerning another of the petty tyrants, that he had exercised great cruelties in slaying, & chopping off the hands and noses of many persons, aswell men as women, and destroying very much people.

Another time the captaine sent the self same cruell man with certaine Spaniardes into the Prouince of Bogata, to bee informed by the inhabitants what Lorde it was, that was successour vnto the chiefe Lordze, whom he had made to die ye cruell death in those tozments spoken of before: Who running along the countrie throughout sundzie places, tooke as many Indians as he could come by: And for that he could not learn of them, what he was that succeeded that Lozde, he mangled off some handes, he did cast others, men and women vnto hungrie mastiues, who rend them in peeces. And in this maner haue been destroyed very many Indies, and Indesses. One time at the fourth watch of the night, he went to ouerrunne Caciks or gouernours of the lande, with many of the Indians, which were in peace, and helde themselues assured (for he had giuen them his faith, & assurance that they shoulde receiue no harme nor damage) vpon credit whereof, wherof, they were come foorth of their holes in the mountains, where they had been hid, to people the plaine, in the which stoode their citie: thus being commen without suspicion, & trusting the assurance made, he tooke a great number, aswell men as womē, and commanded to holde out their handes stretched against the ground, & hinselfe with a woodknife cut of their hands, telling them that he did on them this chastisement, for that they woulde not confesse, where their new Lorde was, which had succeeded in the charge of gouernement of the Realme,

Another time for that the Indians gaue him not a cofer full of golde, that this cruel captaine required them: he sent men to warre vpon them: who cut off the handes and noses of men and women without number. They cast others before their dogs being hunger bitten, and vsed to the feate of feeding on flesh, the which dispatched and deuoured them.

Another time the Indians of that Realme perceiuing, that the Spaniards had brent 3. or 4. of their principall Lordes, they fled for feare vp into a mountaine, from whence they might defende themselues against their enemies so estraunged from all humanitie. There were of them by the testimonie of the witnesses a foure or fiue thousande Indians. This aboue saide Captaine sent a great and notable tyrant, which exceeded farre most of those to whom he had giuen the charge to ransacke and waste, together with a certaine number of Spaniardes, to the ende that they should chastise the Indian rebels: as they would seeme to make them for that they were fled from a pestilence & slaughter so intollerable: and as though it apperteined vnto them, to chastice and punish them as malefactors themselues in deede being worthie of all torment without that any body should haue of them pitie or compassion, being so deuoid thereof, as appeareth by the handling of those poore innocents of that fashion. Well, so it is that the Spanish by force preuailed to get vppe to the mountaine: for the Indians were naked without weapons. And the Spaniardes cryed peace vnto the Indians: assuring them, that they would do them no harme: and that they of their partes shoulde not war any longer. Streight way as the Indians stinted from their owne defense, the vile cruel man sent to ye

Spani-

Spaniardes to take the fortes of the mountaine, and when they shoulde get them to enclose within them the Indians. They set then like vnto Tigers and Lions, vpon these lambes so meeke, and put them to the edge of the sworde, so long that they were faine to breath and rest themselues. And after hauing rested a certaine season, the captaine commaunded that they shoulde kill and cast downe from the mountaine, the which was very highe, the residue that were aliue: that which was done. And these witnesses say, that they sawe as it were a cloude of the Indians cast downe from the mountaine, to the number by estimation of seuen hundreth men together, where they fell battered to peeces.

And to atchieue all his great crueltie, they searched al the Indians that were hid amongst the bushes: and hee commaunded to cut of their heads, at blockes ends: and so they slue them and cast them downe the mountaine: yet coulde not hee content him selfe with those saide thinges so cruell, but that hee would make himselfe a litle better knowne, augmenting his horrible sinnes, when as hee commaunded that all the Indians men and wome, which some priuate persons had taken aliue (for euery one in those massacres is accustomed to cull out some one or other mankinde and womankind, to the ende to become his seruants) shoulde be put into a strawen house, sauing and reseruing those, which seemed necessarie to bee employed in their seruice, and that there shoulde be put to fire: thus were there burned fourty or fiftie. Hee caused the rest to bee sloug to the carrion kinde dogges, which rende them in peeces, and deuoured them.

Another time the selfe same tyrant went to a Citie called Cotta, and tooke there a great number of Indians, and caused to be dismembred by his dogs, a fifteene or twentie Lordes of the principal, and cut the handes of a great multitude of men & women: which saide handes hee hanged one by another on a pole, to the ende the other Indians might see that, which he had done vnto them. There were so hanged one by another threescore and ten payre of hands. He slyped off besides from many women and children their noses.

No creature liuing and reasonable, is able to decipher the mischiefes

mischiefes and cruell dealings of this fellowe, enemie of God. For they are without number, neuer otherwise hearde of, nor seene: those, I meane, which he hath done in the lande of Guatimala, and all about where he hath become, for there are a good many yeres passed, in the which he hath bene professed in the misterie, to bereaue that land, & those people.

The witnesses say for a surcharge, that the cruell dealings & slaughters which haue beene committed, and are yet in the saide Realme of new Grenado, by the captaines themselues in person and by their consents giuen vnto all the other tyrants, wasters, and weeders of the nature of man, which were in his company, and the which hath laid all the countrie wilde & waste, are suche and so excessiue, that if his maiestie doe not take some order therein in some time (albeit that the slaughter and discomfiture of ý Indians is done only to bereaue thē of their gold, the which they haue none of, for they haue surrendred all that which they had) they wil in a short time make an end of them so in such sort, that there will bee no more Indians to inhabite the lande, but that it wyll remaine in a wildernesse without beeing manured.

Nay, wee must note heere the cruell and pestilent tyrannie of these cursed tyrants, howe raging and diuelish it hath beene, that in the space of two or three peeres, sithence that this realme hath bene first discouered (which as they say both those that haue been there, and those which depose as witnesses, was the moste peopled of inhabitantes, as possiblie might bee any Countrie in the worlde,) they haue rased and emptied it with slaughters, declaring themselues so farre remooued from pittie, and the reuerent feare of God and the Prince, that the opinion is, without the present succour of his Maiestly, to stay these vnnatural & diuelish tyrannies, there wil not remaine as muche as one man aliue, & I verily beleue it. For I haue seen with mine own eyes that in these parts, they haue destroyed and dispeopled in a small time, great countries.

There are other great Prouinces, which bounde vpon the saide Realme, of newe Grenado, which they call Popayan and

Cali

Cali, and three or foure others, which containe more then 500. leagues of ground, which they haue destroyed and desolated in the same maner, as they haue done others, robbing and slaying with torments, and the enormities afore spoken of. For the land is very fertile, and those that come from thence now dayly, doe report, ỹ it is a rufull thing to see so manie goodly townes burned and layd desolate, as they might behold passing vp & downe that way: so as there, where there was wont to be in one towne a thousand or two thousand housholdes, they haue not founde fiftie, and the rest vtterly ransacked and dispeopled. And in some quarters they haue found two or three hundred leagues of lande dispeopled and burned, & great cities destroyed. And finally, by that, that sithence into the Realmes of Peru, of the Prouince side of Quito, are entred farre into the Countrie sore and fel tyrants, as far as to the said Realme of Grenado, & of Popayan, & of Cali by the coast of Carthagene, and Araba, & other accursed tyrants of Carthagene haue gone to assault Quito, and more ouer, afterwards of the riuer side of S. John, which is on ỹ south side, all the whiche haue met to ioyne handes together in this exployte: they haue rooted out and dispeopled aboue sixe hundred leagues of land, with the losse of an infinitie of soules, doing still the selfe same to the poore wretches that remain behind, howsoeuer innocent they appeare to be.

Thus then is the rule which I set down at the beginning, by them verified: that is, that the tyrannie, rage, and vngraciousnesse of the Spanishe, hath alwayes proceeded encreasing in their crueltie, vnnaturalnesse, and mischiuousnes amongst those so sweete lambes. That which is continued at this present day in those Prouinces, amongst other their doings worthy the fire and torment, is this which followeth.

After the ends of the slaughters and massacres of the warres, they bring the people into the horrible bondage aboue saide, and giue them to the commaundment of Diuels, to one an hundred Indians, to another three hundred. The commaunder Diuel commandeth, that there come before him an hundred Indians, which incontinent present themselues like lambes. He causing a forty or fiftie amongest them to haue their heads cut off: saith vnto the other there present, I will serue you of the same sauce, if you doe not mee good seruice, or if so be, that you goe out of my sight without my leaue.

That for the honour of God, all they that haue read this peece of worke, or shall giue it a reading, consider nowe, whether this act, so hideous, fell and vnnatural, doe not exceede all crueltie and iniquitie, that may bee imagined, and whether the Spaniardes haue any wrong offered them when a man calleth them Diuels, & whether were better, to giue the Indias to keep to the diuels in hel, or the Spaniards which are at the Indies.

After this I will rehearse another diuelish part, the which I cannot tell whether it be lesse cruell & deuoide of manhood, then are those of sauage beastes: that is, that the Spanish which are in the Indies, doe keepe certaine dogges most raging, taught and trayned wholy to the purpose, to kill and rende in peeces the Indias. That let all those ý are true christians, yea, and also those which are not so, behold, if euer there were the like thinge in the whole worlde : that is, to feed those dogs, they led about wt them wheresoeuer they goe a great nūber of Indians in chaines as if they were hogs, and kill them, making a shambles of mans flesh. And the one of them will say to another, Lend mee a quarter of a villaine, to giue my dogs some meate, vntill I kyll one nexte, altogether as if one shoulde borrowe a quarter of an hog or mutton. There bee others which goe foorth a hunting in the morning with their curres, the which being returned to eat, if another aske him: Howe haue yee sped to day, they aunswere, very well: for I haue killed with my dogs to day, fiftee ne or twentie viliacoes, All these Diabolicall doings, with others like haue beene proued in the sutes of law, that the tyrants haue had one of them against another. Is there any case more ouglie or vnnaturall?

I will here now deport me of this discourse, vntill such time, ý there come other newes of things, in vngraciousnes more notorious and remarkable (if it so be, ý there can be any more greeuous) or vntill such time as wee may returne thither to beholde them our selues anewe, as wee behold them for the space of 42. yeeres continually with mine owne eyes: Protesting in a good conscience before God, that I doe beleeue, and I holde it for

certaine

certaine, that the damages and losses are so great, with the destructions and ouerthrowes of Cities, massacres and murders, with the cruelties, horrible and ougly, with the rauins, iniquities and robberies, all the which things haue beene executed amongest those people, and are yet dayly committed in those quarters: that in all the things, which I haue spoken and deciphered, as I was able the neerest to the truth: I haue not saide one of a thousande, of that which hath beene done, and is dayly a doyng at this present, be it that you consider the qualitie, or bee it, that ye consider the quantitie.

And to the end that all Christians haue the greater compassion of those poore innocents, and that they complaine with mee the more their perdition and destruction, and that they detest the greedinesse, loftinesse, and felnesse of the Spanish: that all doe holde it for a most vndoubted veritie, with all that hath beene aboue saide, that sithence the first discouery of the Indies vntyll nowe, the Indians neuer did harme vnto the Spanishe in any place wheresoeuer, vntill suche time, that they firste receiued wrongs and iniuries, being robbed and betrayed: but indeede did repute them to be immortall, supposing them to bee descended from heauen, and they receiued them for suche, vntill suche time as that they gaue it forth manifestly to be knowen by their doings, what they were, and whereto they tended.

I will adioyne heereunto this, that from the beginning vnto this houre, the Spaniardes haue had no more care to procure that vnto those people shoulde bee preached the faith of Iesus Christe, then as if they had been curre dogs, or other beastes: but in lien thereof, which is much worse, they haue forbidden by expresse meanes the religious men to doe it, for because that that seemed vnto them an hinderance likely to bee, to the getting of their golde, and these riches which their auarice foreglutted in. And at this day there is no more knowledge of God throughout the Indies, to wit, whether hee bee of tymber, of the ayre, or the earth, then there was an hundred yeeres agoe, excepting newe Spaine, whether the religious men haue gone, which is but a litle corner of the Indies: and so are they perished, and doe perishe all without faith, and without sacraments.

I brother

I brother Bartholomewe delas Caſas oʒ Caſaus, religious of the oʒder of S. Dominicke, which by the mercie of God am come into this courte of Spayne, to ſewe that the hell might bee withdʒawen from the Indes, and that these innumerable soules, redeemed by the blood of Jesus Chʒiſt, ſhoulde not periſhe foʒ euermoʒe without remedie, but that they might knowe their creatoʒ and bee saued: also foʒ the care and compaſſion that I haue of my countrey, which is Caſtile, to the ende that God deſtroy it not foʒ the great ſinnes thereof, committed against the fayth and his honour, and against our neighbours: foʒ certaine mens ſakes notablie zealous of the gloʒy of God, touched with compaſſion of the afflictions and calamities of others, followers of this court: howebeit, that I was purposed to do it, but I could not so soone haue done it, because of my continuall occupations, I atchieued this treatise and ſummarie at Ualencia, the 8. of December, 1542. the foʒce beeing mounted to the highest type of extremitie, and all the violences, tyrannies, desolations, anguiſhes, and calamities abouesayde, ſpʒead ouer all the Indies, where ther are any Spaniardes, although they bee moʒe cruell in one part then they bee in an other, and moʒe sauage, and moʒe abhominable.

Mexico and her confines are leſſe euill intreated. In truth, there they can not execute their outrages openly, foʒ that there and not elſewhere, there is ſome foʒme of iuſtice, as ſlender as it is. Foʒ because that there also they kill them with diueliſhe tributes: I am in good hope, that the Emperour and King of Spayne, our liege Soueraigne Loʒde, don Charles the fifte of that name, who beginneth to haue vnderſtanding of the miſchieues and treaſons that there haue been, and are committed against those pooʒe peeple, against the will of God, and his owne, (foʒ they haue alwayes cunningly concealed the trueth from him) will roote out those euilles, and take ſome oʒder foʒ this newe woʒlde that God hath giuen him, as vnto one that loueth and doeth iuſtice: whoſe honour and pʒoſperous eſtate Imperiall, God almightie vouchſafe to bleſſe with long life, foʒ the benefite of his whole vniuerſall Church, and to the saluation of his

owne

owne royall soule. Amen.

After hauing couched in writing the premisses, I vnderstood of certayne lawes and ordinaunces, whiche his Maiestie hath made about this time at Barcellone, Anno. 1542. in the moneth of Nouember, and the yeere following at Madrill: by the which ordinaunces, there is order set downe, as the case them seemeth to require : to the end, to cut off the mischeieues and sinnes whiche are committed against God and our neighbours, tending to the vtter ruine & perdition of this new world, His Maiestie hath made these lawes, after hauing holde many assemblies of persons of authoritie, of learning and conscience, and after hauing had disputations and conferences in Ualladolyd: and finally with the assent and aduise of al those others which haue giuen their aduise in writing, and haue been founde neerest approching vnto the law of Iesus Christ, and withall free from the corruption and soyle of the treasures robbed from the Indians : the which treasures haue soyled the handes and much more the soules of many, ouer whom those treasures and auarice haue got the maisterie, and where hence hath proceeded the blinding, which hath caused so to marre all without remorse. These lawes being published, the creatures of those tyrantes, who then were at the court, drew out sundrie coppes thereof (for it grieued them at the hearts : for that it seemed them that thereby there was a doore shut vp vnto them agaynst their rauine and extortion afore rehearsed) and dispersed them into diuers quarters of the Indies. Those which had the charge to robbe, roote out, and consume by their tyrannies, (euen as they had neuer kept any good order but rather disorder, such as Lusifer himselfe might haue helde)as they read those coppies before the new iudges might come to execute their charge, knowing it (as it is sayd, and that very crediblie) by those who vntill this time haue supported and mayntayned their crimes and outrages, to be likely that such execution shoulde bee vsed of those laws : they ran into a mutinie in such wise, as that when the good Iudges were come to doe their duties, they aduised with them selues (as those which had lost the feare and loue of God)to cast off also all shame, and obedience which they owe to the king, and so tooke vnto them the name of open and arrant

tray-

traytours, behauing them ſelues as moſt cruell and graceleſſe
tyzantes: and principally in the realme of Peru, where preſent-
ly this yeere 1442. are committed actes ſo horrible and frightfull, as neuer were the like, neither in the Indies, nor in all the
worlde beſides, not onely agaynſt the Indians, the which all or
in a maner all are ſlayne, all thoſe regions being diſpeopled: but
alſo betwixt themſelucs by a iuſt iudgement of God, who hath
permitted that they ſhoulde bee the butchers one of an other of
them. By meanes of the ſupport of this rebellion, none of all the
other partes of this newe worlde would obey thoſe lawes: But
under colour of making ſupplication to his Maieſtie to the contrary, they haue made an inſurrection aſwell as the others. For
that it irketh them to leaue their eſtates and goodes whiche they
haue vſurped, and to vnbinde the handes of the Indians, whome
they detayne in a perpetuall captiuitie. And there where they
ceaſe to kill with the ſwoorde, redily and at the inſtant, they kill
them a little and a little, by perſonall ſlaueries, and vniuſt charges and intollerable. That which the king could not hitherunto
let: for becauſe that they all, great and litle, roue and robbe, ſome
moze, ſome leſſe: ſome ouertly, and ſome couertly, and vnder the
pretence of ſeruing the king: diſhonour God, and rob the king.

M 4   The

The Authour his wordes farder to *king Philip*, then at the time of writing thereof, Prince of *Spayne*.

THat which followeth hereafter immediatly : is a part of a Miſſiue or letter ſent, written by one, who him ſelfe was a partie in theſe voiages : recounting the works the which a captayne did, and conſented to the dooing in the countrey, all the way as hee paſſed. And albeit ſo, that the ſaide miſſiue being put to binding in one booke with other papers, the binder eyther forgot, or loſt a leaſe or two : notwithſtanding, foraſmuch as the ſaid miſſiue contayned things fearefull, euen to aſtoniſhement, the which one of them that had done them had giuen me : and that I had them all in my keeping : I thought good to preſent you therwithall, ſuch as it is nowe, though without beginning or ending. For that this fragment remayning of the whole , is full of notable pointes : and therefore being reſolued that it ſhoulde bee ſo printed, truſting that it will cauſe no leſſe compaſſion and horror in your highneſſe minde, then the other matters afore mentioned, with a deſire forthwith to prouide for the redreſſe.

The Miſſiue.

Ee gaue licence to put them to the Chaine and in bondage : That which they did : and the Captayne led after him three or foure droues of theſe perſons enchayned : and in this doing, he procured not ẏ the countrey ſhoulde bee inhabited and peopled (as had been conuenient ſhoulde haue been

been done) but robbing from the Indians all their victuals they
had, the inbornes of the countrey were reduced to suche an extremitie, that there were founde great numbers dead of famine
in the high wayes. And the Indians comming and going too
and fro the coast, laden with the carriage of the Spaniardes, hee
was the death by these meanes of about ten thousande. For not
one that arriued at the very coast escaped death : by reason of
the excessiue heate of the countrey.

After this following the same tract and way, by the whiche
John of Ampudia was gone, hee sent the Indians which hee
had purchased in Quito, a day before him, to the ende they should
discouer the bourges of the Indians, and should pillage them,
that when hee came with his maynie, hee might finde his bootie readie.

And those Indians were his owne mates : of the whiche
such a one had two hundred, such a one three hundred, and suche
a one a hundred : according to the baggage that euery one of
them had: which Indians came to yeelde them selues to their
maisters with all ý they had robbed. At dooing whereof they
committed great cruelties towarde young children and women:
and so had hee vsed before to doe in Quito, in burning the whole
countrey, and namely the garners where the Lordes kept their
Mahis in prouision.

Hee suffered to bee done great outrages, in slaying the
sheepe with the which they nourished and entertayned for the
most part, both the Spanishe, and the naturall inhabitauntes of
the countrey. And onely to haue the braynes and the sewet, hee
permitted that there shoulde bee killed two or three hundred
wethers, of the whiche the flesh was fayne to bee cast away.
And the Indians friendes to the Spaniardes, and the whiche
went with the Spaniardes, onely to eate the sheepes hearts, killed a great number, for as much as they eate none other thing.

And two men in one prouince, named Purua, killed 25. wethers and sheep fit for carriage like our horse, & the which were
worth amongst the Spaniardes twentie, and fiue and twentie
duckates a peece, only to haue to eate the braines, and the sewet.
So as by this disorder of exceeding slaughter of beastes, haue

been

been loſt aboue an hundꝛed thouſande head of cattell. By occaſion where of alſo, the countrey came into a great neceſſitie : the
natiue of the lande miſerablie dying of famine. And Quito,
which was furniſhed of ſo great ſtoꝛe of Mahis, that it can not
bee well ſpoken: was by this meanes ſo aſſaulted with famaine,
that a ſtrike oꝛ buſhell of Mahis, was rayſed to the pꝛiſe of 10.
Buckets, and a ſheepe to as muche.

After that the ſayde Captaine was returned from the coaſt,
hee determined to depart from Quito, and to goe ſeeke the Captayne John de Ampudia, leauing thereto moe then two hundꝛed
of foote men and hoꝛſe men, amongſt whome were a great many
inhabitauntes of the citie of Quito. Unto thoſe inhabitaunts the
captaine gaue licence to carrie with them the Cacikes, that were
eſcheated them in ſharing, with as many Indians as they would.
That which they did : and Alfonſo Sanches Nutta caried foꝛth
with him his Cacike, with moe then an hundꝛed Indians beſids:
and in like maner Peter Cibo and his couſin: and they led out
moꝛe then an hundꝛed and fiftie with their wiues: and ſundꝛie alſo ſped out their childꝛen, becauſe that in a maner euery one died
foꝛ hunger. Alſo Moꝛan inhabitant of Popaian, caried out moe
then two hundꝛed perſons. And the like did all the reſt, citizens
and ſouldiers, euery one after his abilitie : the ſouldiers crauing
that they might haue licence giuen them to captiue thoſe Indians men and women, which they carried foꝛth : the which was
graunted vnto them vntyll the death of the ſayde captiues, and
thoſe deceaſed, to take as many moꝛe : foꝛ if the Indians were
ſubiectes of his Maieſtie, ſo likewiſe were the Spaniardes tᵭat
died in the warres as well as they.

And after this maner departed the ſayde Captayne of Quito, going to a citie called Otaba, the which he held at that houre
foꝛ his ſhare: and demanded of the Cacike, that there ſhoulde bee
giuen him fiue hundꝛed men to lead to the warres : which were
giuen him with certayne pꝛincipall perſons of the Indians. Hee
departed ſome of thoſe people amongſt his ſouldiers, and ledde
foꝛth the reſt with hun, ſome laden, and ſome chayned, and ſome
vnbounde to ſerue him, and to bꝛing him meate.

Thus

Thus carried hee his souldiers some pinniond in chaynes, and some in coardes. When they departed out of the Prouince of Quito, they carried out moe then sixe thousande Indians, men and women, and of al those there neuer returned home into their countrey twentie persons. For they dyed all thorough the great and excessiue trauell, which they made them endure in those broiling countreys contrary to their nature. It happened at that tyme that one Alfonso Sanches, whom the saide Captayne sent for chieftayne ouer a certayne number of men into a Prouince there, met with a good company of women, and young boyes laden with victuals: who stayed wayting for them without mouing from the place to giue them of that which they had, and hauing so done, the captaine commaunded that they should bee put to the sharpe of the sworde. There happened here a maruailous thing: which was, that a souldier striking an Indesse woman, his sworde brake a two in the middest, at the first blowe, and at the seconde blowe there remayned nought in his handes, but the pomell hauft without that the woman was hurt. And an other souldier, willing to strike another Indesse woman, with a square dagger he had, the dagger brake at the first choppe, the length of foure fingers, and at the seconde, there remayned vnto him no more saue the hauft.

At the same tyme the sayde Captayne yeeded foorth of Quito, and drewe out a great number of the naturall inbornes, vnmarriyng them, and giuing their young wiues vnto his Indians whom hee ledde along, and the others wiues hee gaue to others which remayned in the citie, for that they were too olde.

There followed out of Quito a woman with a litle childe in her armes, crying after him, and entreating him, that her husbande might not bee forced to goe with him, for that shee had three little children, the whiche shee coulde not nourishe but were ready to dye for hunger:

And as the Captayne gaue her a churlishe answere at her first sute, shee returned the seconde time with greater cries, saying, that her children dyed for hunger.

And

And seeing that the Captayne gaue her the repulse, and that hee woulde not restore her, her husbande: shee beat the childes head agaynst the stones, and slue it.

It came to passe also, that at the tyme that the sayde Captayne came into the prouice of Lili, to a towne called Palo neere vnto the great riuer, where hee founde the Captayne John de Ampudia, which was gone before to discouer, and pacifie the countrey: the saide Ampudia kepte a citie by him prouided of a garrisō in the name of his maiesty, and of the marques Fraūcis of Pizarro: and had set ouer them for gouernours ordinarie, one Petre Solano of Quemoues, and 8. counsellours, & all the rest of the countrey was in peace & shared out amongst them. And as he knew that the sayd captaine was in the said riuer, he came to see him with a great number of the inhabitantes of the countrey, and peaceful Indians, laden with victuals and fruites. Shortly after also all the neighbour Indians came to see him, bringing him food. There were the Indians of Lamundi, and of Palo, and of Soliman, and of Bolo.

Nowe because that they brought no Mahis which he would haue, hee sent a great number of Spaniardes with their Indians, to go search for Mahis: commaunding them to bring some wheresoeuer they founde any. So went they to Bolo, and to Palo, and founde the Indians men and women in their housen in peace: and the sayd Spaniards with those that were with them, twoke them and robbed their Mahis, their golde and coverings, and all that they had, and bounde many.

The Indians seeing that they entreated them so euill, went to complaine vnto the sayde Captayne, requesting that all which had been bereft them, might be restored them: But the Captain woulde restore them none, and forbidde them to come at him any more. Notwithstanding foure or fiue dayes after the Spaniardes eftsoones returne to fetche Mahis, and to pilladge the Indians natiue of the soyle as before time. Wherefore, they seeing that the Captayne kepte no faith with them: all the Countrie arose and revolted from the Spanishe, whereof ensued greate dammage, and GOD and the

kings maiestie offended : and by this meanes the countrie re=
mained dispeopled:for y the Dlomas & the Hanipos their ene=
mies which are mostaine people,& warlike,descended dayly to
take and rob them,when they perceiued the citie and places of
their abode left destitute. And amongst them, hee who was the
stronger,did eate vp his fellowe,for all dyed for famine. This
done,the captaine came to the citie of Ampudia,where hee was
receiued for generall,and seuen dayes after from thence hee de=
parted to goe towards the harbour of Lili and Peti, with more
then two hundred horsmen and footemen . After this,that saide
is,the saide, chiefe gouernour sent his captaines of one side and
other,to bid cruell battayle to the natiue Indias:slaying a great
number of them as wel men as women:burning also their hou=
ses,and spoling their goods. This indured a good many dayes.
And the saide captaine was gone towardes a citie named Yce,
withall the Indians whome they had taken in Lili, without re=
leasing any one : and beeing come to the saide Yce, hee sent in=
continent Spaniardes to pilladge,take and slay all the Indians
men and women,that they coulde take : thus they burned moe
then an hundred. From this place they goe to a Citie called
Tukilicui, from whence the Cacike of the place yeeded foorth
incontinent in peace, a number of Indians going before him.
The captaine demaunded golde of him and of his Indians. The
Cacik told him that hee had but a small deale, and that whiche
he had should be giuen him: & immediatly al began to giue him
all that they had. Whereupon the sayde captaine gaue vnto
euery of them a ticket,with the name of the saide Indian for a
testimoniall that hee had giuen him golde : affirming that hee
which shoulde haue neuer a ticket, should bee cast to the dogs
to bee deuoured, because hee gaue him no golde. Whereupon
the Indians for feare y they were put in,gaue him all the gold
that they were able : & those which had none fled into the mountaines and other townes for feare to be slaine. By reason whereof perished a great number of the natiue inhabitants of the cou=
trie. And shortly after the said captaine commanded the Cacike
to sende two Indians to another citie named Dagua , to will
them that they shoulde come in peace,and bring him golde in a=

boundance

bundance. And comming to another citie, he sent that night ma¬
ny Spaniardes to take the Indians, and namely of Tulilicui.
So as they brought the next morrow aboue an hundred persons:
and all those which could beare burdens, they tooke them for the
selues, and for their souldiers, and put them to the chaine, wher¬
of they dyed all. And the saide captaine gaue the little children
vnto the said Cacik Tulilicui that hee should eate them: and in
truth the skinnes of those children are kept in the house of the
saide Cacik Tulilicui full of ashes: and so departed hee from
thence without an interpreter, and went towardes the Prouin¬
ces of Calile, where he ioyned himselfe vnto the captaine John
de Ampudia, who had sent him to discouer another way, dooing
both of them great outrages, and much mischiefe vnto the inha¬
bitants of the countrie where they became. And the said John
de Ampudia came vnto a Citie, the Cacik and Lorde whereof
called Bitacur had caused to make certaine ditches to defende
himselfe, and there fell into the same two horses, the one of An¬
tonie Rodondos, the other of Marc Marquesis. That of Mar¬
cos Marquis died, the other not. For which cause the said Am¬
pudia commaunded to take all the Indians men and women
that might be: And therupon tooke & laid together more then an
hundred persons, whome they cast aliue into those ditches and
slue them, and brent withal more then an hundred houses in the
said citie, And in that maner met in a great Citie, where with¬
out sommoning (the Indians being at peace, and without anye
spokesman to goe betweene them,) they slue with their speares
a great number of them, making on them mortall warre. And
as it is said, soone after they were met, the saide Ampudia tolde
the Captaine what hee had done in Bitaco, and howe hee cast so
many into the ditches: and the sayd captaine aunswered, that it
was well done, and that he for his part had done as much at the
riuer of Bamba when hee entred the same, which is in the Pro¬
uince of Quito, and that hee had slong into the ditches moe then
two hundred persons, and there they stayed warring on all the
countrie. Soone after hee entred into the Prouince of Bitu, or
Anzerma: in making cruell warre with fire and blood till they
came

came as farre as vnto the salt houses. And from thence,hee sent Frauncis Garcia before him to pilladge,who made cruel warre on the naturall inhabitants of the Countrie as hee had done before him. The Indians came vnto him two and two, making signes,that they demaunded peace on the behalfe of the whole Countrie: alleadging that they woulde afoord him,all that hee coulde reasonably demaund,were it golde,or women, or victuals, only that they woulde not kill them, as indeede it was a troth. For themselues afterwardes confessed it to be so.But the saide Frauncis Garcia,bid them get them packing: Telling them moreouer that they were a sort of drunkardes, and that he vnder stood them not,and so returned hee to the place where the saide Captaine was,and they made a complot, to ouerrunne all the Prouince,making cruell warre on all the Countrie,in spoiling,robbing,and slaying all: and with the souldiers,which hee brought with him drewe thence moe then two thousand soules, and all those dyed in the chaine. Before departing the place which he had peopled,they slue moe then fiue hundred persons. And so returned to the Prouince of Calili. And by the way if any Inde or Indesse were weary,in such sort that they could not passe any further,they did incontinently head them, paring it off from the shoulders euen with the chaine,to the ende not to take the paines to open the locke thereof: and to the end that others which went the same way shoulde not make wise to be sicke,and by this meanes dyed they all: and in the high wayes were lefte all those people whichhe made his purchase of out of Quito,& of Pasto,and of Quilla Cangua,and of Para,and of Popayan, and of Lili,and of Cali, andof Anzerma, and a great number of people dyed. Also immediately vpon theyr returne vnto the great Citie, they entred into it,slaying all that they could: taking in that day moe then three hundreth persons.

Hee sent from the Prouince of Lili, the saide Captaine John de Ampudia, with very manye souldiers vnto the lodgynges and peopled places of Lili: to the ende that they shoulde take all the Indes and Indesses they coulde: And that they shoulde bring them vnto him to serue for loadyng:

for

for becauſe that al thoſe which he brought him before time from Anzerma & from Alli, were dead, whiche were great numbers. And the ſaide John de Ampudia brought moe then a thouſande perſons, and ſlue very many. The captaine thus tooke as many as he needed to ſerue his turne, and gaue the reſt vnto the ſouldiers, which confined them to the chayne in whiche they dyed. So diſpeopling the ſaid citie of Spaniardes and inbornes of the countrie, both in ſo great a number, as appeareth by the fewneſſe of the folke, that are remanent: he departed thence to goe to Popayan, & left in the way a Spaniarde named Martine Aguirr, who was not able to follow the reſt. And beeing come to Popayan, he placed there a garriſon, and began to root out and rob thoſe Indians there, in the order that he had kept elſwhere. And hee erected there a mynt royall, melting all the golde hee coulde come by, with all that, that John de Ampudia had before he came vnto him, and without keeping any other audit or reckoning, and without giuing any part to any ſouldier, taking the whole to his owne vſe, except a little as came in his head to giue vnto ſuch as had loſt theyr horſes. And this done, bereauing the kings Maieſtie of his fiſt part, ſaid he went to Cuſto, there to giue in his account and audit vnto the gouernour. But in deede he went to Quito, taking by the way very many Indians, men and women, which all dyed by the way, or at the place at Quito. Ouer and beſides that, he altered the copne royall of the mynt, which he had made. Here is to be remembred a word, which this man ſpake of himſelfe, as one not ignorant of ſo many euils and miſchieues, which he wrought. Fiftie yeres hence, thoſe the which ſhall paſſe by this way, and heere ſpeake of theſe things, ſhall ſay, This way went a Tyrant

Your highnes may know and be well aſſured, that theſe entries and aſſaults made vnto theſe realmes, and this maner of viſiting the Indians, which liued in ſecuritie in their regions, and the vngracicouſneſſe which he did in thoſe ſame, haue been practiſed and executed by the Spaniards, which haue alwayes followed the ſame traine and maner of doing, from the time that they firſt began to diſcouer vnto this preſent day, throughout all the Indes.

To the Reader.

Mong diuers the remedies by Fryar *de las Casas* Bishop of the royal towne called *Chiapa*, propounded in the assembly of sundrie prelates named Parsons, by his maiesties commandement gathered together in the towne of *Valladolid* the yeere of our Lord 1 542. for order and reformation to bee obserued in the Indies : the eight in order was this insuing, which consisteth vpon twentie reasons & motions, whereupō he did cōclude, *That the Indies ought not to be giuen to the Spaniardes in Commendam, fee farme, or vasselage, neither vnder any other title whatsoeuer : if his maiestie will according to his desire ease them of such tyrannies and losses as they doe susteine, deliuering them as it were out of the Dragons throate: least they doe wholy consume and slay thē, & so all that world remaine desart & voide of the naturall inhabitants, wherewith we haue seene it replenished.*

THe eight remedie , is among all other principall and most in force, as without which all the rest are to no purpose, for that they all haue relatio n therunto, as euery motion to his proper end, in whatsoeuer toucheth or is of any importaunce vnto your Maiestie, which no man can expresse: in as much as therupon dependeth at the least the whole losse or preseruation of the Indies. And the remedie that I speake of is this, that your Maiestie do determin, decree, cōmand, & solēnely in your soueraigne courts ordein by pragmaticall sactions & royal statuts, ꝑ all the Indies aswell alreadie subdued, as heereafter to bee subdued, may bee inserted, reduced, and incorporate into the royal crowne of *Castile & Leon*, to be holden in chief of your maiestie as free subiects & vassals, as they are . Likewise that they bee not giuen in *commendá* vnto the Spaniards: but that it stand as an inuiolable constitution, determination and royall lawe, that they neuer, neither at this time, neither hereafter in time to come, may bee

alienated

alienated or taken from the saide royall crown, neither that they bee giuen, commanded, demised in fee farme, by depost, commandement or alienatiō, either vnder any other title or maner what soeuer, and bee dismembred from the royall crowne, for any whatsoeuer the seruice or desart of any, either vpon any necessitie that may happen, or for any cause or colour whatsoeuer that may be pretended, For the inuiolable obseruation, or establishement of which law, your maiestie shall formally sweare by your faith, and on your worde and royall crowne, and by all other sacred thinges, whereby Christian Princes doe vsually sweare, that at no time neither your selfe, neither your successours in these 10, Dominions, or in the Indies so farre as in you shall lie, shal reuoke the same: and you shall further set downe in expresse wordes in your royall will and testament, that this decree be euer kept, mainteined, and vpholden: also that so farre as in your self or in them shal lie, they shall cōfirme and continue the same: And for porose of the necessitie hereof, there bee twentie reasons to be alleadged: out of which twentie we haue drawen and put in writing so many as may seeme to serue to our purpose,

Extract out of the second reason.

THE Spaniardes through their great auarice and couetousnes to get, doe not permit any religious persons to enter into their townes and holdes which they possesse, alleadging that they receiue double losse by them. One and the principall is, that religious persons do keepe the Indies occupied when they gather them together to their Sermons, so as in the meane time their worke is omitted, while the Indians being idle, labour not: yea, it hath so fallen out, that the Indians being in the Church at the Sermon, the Spaniarde comming in in the face of all the people, hath taken fiftie, or a hundred, or so many as he hath needed to carry his baggage and stuffe, and such as would not goe, he hath loden with stripes spurning them foorth with his feete, thereby to the great griefe both of the Indians and of the religious persons troubling & molesting all that were present, & so defeating the al of the benefit of their saluatiō, Their other hinderance that

they

they say they doe sufteine, is, that after the Indians are taught & become Christians, they take vppon them as masters, pretending more knowledge then they haue, & therefore will not be so seruiceable as afore.

The Spaniards require no more of the Indians but authority to commaund them, and that they worship them as Gods.

The Spaniards openly and of set purpose, do hinder the course of the gospel, and keepe the Indians from Christendome.

Sometime it falleth so out, that a towne or borow is giuen betweene three or foure Spaniardes, to one more, to another lesse, so as sometime one hath for his portion the husband, another the wife, and the third the childré, as they were swine. Thus doe they possesse the Indians. One appointeth them to labour a peece of lande : another sendeth them to the mines loaden like beastes : another hyreth them by two and two as they were moyles to carry burdens thirtie, fortie, fiftie, a hundred or two hundred miles out right. And this haue we seen to be a daily vse: heereofcommeth, it that the Indians cannot heare Gods word, or bee instructed in Christian faith : they make them of free mé very strange bondslaues. They haue subuerted and dispersed great townes, and a whole worlde of people, so as they haue not left any houses standing together, no not so much as the children with the fathers. The Spaniards make no more account, neither haue any more regard of conuerting the Indians, then if al those reasonable soules should perishe with the bodies, and were not hereafter to receiue immortall life, glory, or paine, no more then beastes.

Out of the thirde reason.

THe Spaniards are charged to instruct the Indians in our holy catholike faith : whereupon on a time when we examined Iohn Colmenere of S. Marthe, a fantastical, ignorant, and foolish man, who had gotten a great towne in *commendam*, and had a charge of soules, he could not tell how to blesse himselfe : and asking him what doctrine he taught the Indians committed to his charge, he said, he gaue thé to the diuell : also that it was enough for

for him to say *Per signum sanctin Cruces.* Howe can the Spaniardes that trauaile to the Indies, howe noble or valiant so euer
they bee, haue any care of the soules, when the most of them
are ignorant of their Creede and ten commandements, & know
not the matters perteining to their owne saluation, neither doe
trauaile to the Indies for any other purpose but to satisfie their
owne desires and couetous affections, being for the most Parte
vicious, corrupt, vnhonest, and disordinate persons : so as he that
would way them in an equal ballance, & compare them with the
Indians, shoulde finde the Indians without comparison, more
vertuous and holy then them. For the Indians what infidels soeuer they bee, doe neuerthelesse keepe them to one and their own
wife, as nature and necessitie teacheth, and yet we see some Spaniarde haue foureteene or more, which Gods commandementes
do forbid. The Indians deuoure no mans goods, they doe no
man wrong: they doe not vexe, trouble, or slay any, where them
selues doe see the Spaniard es commit all sinnes, iniquities; and
treacheries, that man can commit against all equitie and iustice.
To bee briefe, the Indians doe not beleeue any thing, but doe
mocke at all that is shewed them of God, beeing in trueth fully
rooted in this opinion of our God, that he is the worst, the most
vniust, and the most wicked of all Gods, because he hath such seruants; also concerning your maiestie, they thinke you the most
vniust and cruell of all kinges, because you doe both sende thither
and keepe heere such euill subiectes, supposing that your maiestie
doth feed vpon humane flesh and blood. We know these things
to be very new and strange to your highnes, but yet there they
be very vsuall and auncient. Many like matters which with our
eyes we haue seene, might we speake of, but they would be offen-
siue to your maiesties eares, and would besides feare men, forcing
the to wonder that euer God staied so long from plaging Spaine
in the bottomlesse pit. This title, to giue the Indians to the Spaniards in cõmedã, was neuer inuented to any other end but only
to finde occasion to bring them into bondage. One Spaniard being Lorde, or hauing the charge of some towne or village, will
do more harme by his example and wicked life, then a hundred
good religious persons can do good by edifiyng or conuerting.

Out of the fourth reason.

THe Spaniardes hauing authoritie to commaunde, or particular interest in the Indies, can not by reason of their great couetousnes abstaine from afflicting, troubling, disquieting, vexing, or oppressing the Indians, taking away their goodes, landes, wiues, or children, and vsing among them many other kindes of iniquitie, for the which they can haue no redresse, sanction, or warrant at your Maiesties chiefe iustice, because the Spaniardes doe make them afraide: yea sometimes doe kill them, least they shoulde complaine, as wee haue had certaine notice: and thereupon it is euident, that they can haue no rest or quiet, to tende to matters pertaining God, but doe sustaine a thousande lets, anguishes, tormentes, sorowes, afflictions, heauinesses, and cares, hating your Maiestie, and abhorring Gods lawe, which they finde so heauie, bitter, and intollerable: as also your Maiesties yoke and dominion so insupportable, tyrannous, worthie to bee reiected and cast off, that they curse God and fall into desperation, attributing to him all the aforesaide euils, because that vnder the colour and title of his lawe, they do receiue such mishappes, which hee doth beare withall, and doth not correct or chastice those which boasting to be his seruannres, doe put them to all this. They doe night and day mourne after their gods, thinking them to bee better then ours at whom they sustaine suche harmes, while contrarywise of their owne they reape there so many commodities: and there is nothing that troubleth them so much as the Christians,

Out of the fifth reason.

VVE can shewe to your Maiestie, that the Spaniardes haue within 38. or 40. yeeres slaine of iust accompt, aboue 12. Millions of your subiectes: I will not say howe mightily this worlde of people might haue multiplied. This countrey

being,

being the fertileſt, whether for cattel, or mankinde, that is in the worlde: the ſoile being for the moſt part, more temperate and fauourable to humaine generation. All theſe iunumerable perſons, and all theſe people haue the Spaniards ſlaine, to the end to beare ſway, gouerne, & cōmaund ouer the reſt: & when in iniuſt wars they haue ſlaine them, then doe they vſe the reſt, who iuſtly haue withſtood them, in drawing gold & ſiluer, yoking them together like beaſts, to make them carry their burdens, hiring thē & burdening them withall that they can gaine, and liue or die it is all one to them, ſo that they may reape any benefite or coine, I ſpeak but the truth, and yet do leaue out much vnſpoken of that all the world knoweth : and whoſoeuer wꝏlde otherwiſe perſwade your Maieſtie, or would endeuour to excuſe thoſe offences, wee will euen by force of the truth, driue him to knowledge him ſelfe guilty of treaſon, & that he is partaker in theſe murders & roberies committed in the Indies, or els hopeth ſo to be.

What plague of peſtilence, or mortalitie could there haue fallen from heauen that had been able to conſume or make waſt aboue 2500. leagues of flat countrey, repleniſhed with people, and would not haue left either trauailer or inhabitant?

Out of the ſixt reaſon.

THe Spaniardes only for their temporall commoditie, haue blemiſhed the Indies with the greateſt infamie, that any man euen among the moſt horrible and villanous perſons in the world, could be charged withal, & whereby they haue ſought to take thē out of the degree of mankinde: namely that they all were polluted with the abhominable ſinne againſt nature: which is a wretched and falſe ſlaunder. For in all the great Iles, *Hiſpaniola*, *S. Iohn*, *Cuba*, & *Lamaica*: Alſo in the 60. Iles of Lucayos, whiche were inhabited with an infinite nomber of people, the ſame was neuer thought vpon, or once mentioned, as our ſelues can teſtifie, who made diligent inquiſition & ſearch, euen from the beginning. Moreouer, through all Peru, there is no ſuch ſpeach, neither is there any one India throughout ꝥ whole realm of Yucatā ſpotted with that crime, neither generally throughout all thē Indies: ſauing that in ſome other part there is a voice of a few: for whoſe ſakes neuertheles all that world is not to be condemned. We may ſay as much of the eating of mans fleſh, which likewiſe thoſe places that I haue named are free of : although that in other places they do it in deed. They be alſo charged with their idolatrie, as if for being idolaters, men ſhoulde take vpon them to puniſh them, & not referre them to God only, againſt whō they ſin, whiles they haue both lands & dominions ſeuerall to them ſelues, which they hold not of any other thē their natural Lords: beſides that our anceſters were alſo idolaters before the faith was preached vnto them, & that all the world was gathered to Chriſt. The Spaniardes haue purpoſely, & effectually hindered the teaching of the law of God and Ieſus Chriſt : with all other vertues among the Indians, & driuen away the religious perſons out of townes and fortreſſes, leaſt they ſhoulde ſee and diſcloſe their tyrannies: yea, they haue by their euill example, infected & corrupted the Indians, teaching them many odious behauiours and vices, which before they knew not, as blaſpheming the name of Ieſus Chriſt, practiſing of vſerie, lying, & many other abhominations wholy repugnant to their nature. Again, to commit the Indians to the Spaniards, or to leaue them in their handes, is vndoubtedly as much as to giue or leaue them to theſe that will deſtroy & bring them to nought, aſwell in body as ſoule.

The Spaniards hauing fraudulently perſwaded K. Ferdinand, he ſuffered the Indians to be trāſported out of the Iles of Lucayos into Hiſpaniola, and ſo contrary to all reaſon, either naturall or diuine, diſpoſſeſſed them of their own houſes and lands, wherby there periſhed aboue 50000. ſoules: ſo as in aboue 50. Iles, wherof ſome were greater then the Ile of Canary, which before were repleniſhed with people as an Ante heape, afterward there were to be found not aboue eleuen perſons, as our ſelues can teſtifie. To let your Maieſtie vnderſtand the goodnes and vpright dealing of the inhabitants of the ſaide Ilandes called Lucayos : alſo of the ſlaughters, crueltiesies, and ſpoyles that the Spaniardes, theſe good chriſtians made among them, wee might make your royall eares to gloe, and your bowels to lament, and ſo your ſelſe to depart. That the Spaniardes haue warred vpon the Indians, that they haue killed them, taken away their wiues, children, friendes, and kindred : alſo that they haue robbed them of all their goodes, is alreadie sufficiently proued, as also the countrey being vtterly dispeopled and desert, doeth shewe it: the worlde crieth out vpon it: the Angels doe bewaile it, and God himselfe doth dayly teach it vs by the great punishments that he layeth vpon vs.

Out of the seuenth reason.

THe Spaniards doe sucke from the Indians the whole substaunce of their bodies, because they haue nothing else in their houses. They make them spitte blood: They exhibite them to all daungers: They lay vpon them sundrie and intollerable trauailes: and more then al this, They loade them with torments, beatings, and sorowings: To be briefe, they spoile and consume a thousande maner of waies.

To put the Indians into the Spaniardes handes, is, to giue the childes throate to a frantick and mad man when he hath the rasor in his hande : or it is as much as to deliuer men into the power of the furious or capitall enemies, who long time haue verye desiroufly wayted to put them to death. It is as a man shoulde commit a faire young virgin to the guiding of a young man snared, transported, and doting in her loue, whereby shee shoulde be spoiled and deflowred, vnlesse shee were miraculoufly preferued. To be briefe , it were as good to throwe them among the hornes of wilde Bulles, eyther to deliuer them vnto hunger starued Wolues, Lions, and Tygres, and as much good shoulde they gette by any lawes, preceptes, or threates made to the saide hungrie beastes, for the forbidding of them to deuoure them, as much do we say and affirme will any lawes , threates, or preceptes, stay the Spaniardes, when they haue authoritie ouer the Indians from murdering them for their golde. Yea by great and long experience that we haue, wee doe certifie your highnesse, that notwithstanding you shoulde commaunde to set vp a Gibbet before euery Spaniardes gate, and sweare by your Crowne, that for the first Indian that shoulde be missed or slain, you woulde haue them all hanged, yet would they not for feare thereof abstaine from slaying the Indians , in case your Maiestie should graunt or giue them supreme power and authoritie ouer
them,

them, or otherwife howefoeuer.

Out of the eight reafon.

BEfides all that the Indians doe indure in feruing and pleafing
the Spaniarde, there is yet a butcher or cruell hangman, to
keepe them in awe appointed in euery towne and place, and is
tearmed *Eftanciero* or *Calpifque* : who hath authoritie to lay
his clawes vpon them, and to make them labour, and doe what
the Lorde Commaunder, or chiefe thiefe will. So as if in hell,
there were no other torment, yet were this incomparable. This
hangman whippeth them, hee ladeth them with ftripes, hee ba-
fteth them with fcalding greafe, he afflicteth them with continuall tormentes and trauelles, he forceth & defloureth their daughters and wiues, difhonouring and abufing them : hee deuoureth
their hennes whiche are their greateft treafure , not bee-
caufe them felues doe eate them, but that of them they offer pre-
fents and feruice to their greateft Lorde and chiefe tyrant : hee
vexeth them with innumerable other tormentes and griefes : &
leaft they fhoulde complaine of fo many iniuries and miferies,
this tyrant putteth them in feare, faying : that he will accufe
them, and fay that he fee them commit idolatrie. To be briefe,
they muft pleafe and content aboue twentie difordinate and
vnreafonable perfons : fo as they haue foure Lordes and
maifters. Your Maieftie, their Cacique, him that hath them in
commendam, and the *Eftanciero* of whom I laft fpake, whiche
Eftanciero is to them more grieuous to beare then a quintall of
lead, among which we may alfo in truth adde all the *Mochachos*
and *Mores*, that do ferue the commander and mafter, for they al
do moleft, oppreffe, and robbe thefe poore people.

Out of the tenth reafon.

IT is greatly to be feared, leaft God will lay Spain defolate, euen
for thofe horrible finnes that this nation hath committed in the
Indies, whereof we do euidently beholde the fcorge, and all the
world doth fee & confeffe that already it hangeth ouer our heads,
wherwith God doth afflict & fhew that he is highly offeded in
thofe parts through the great deftruction and waft of thofe nations, in that of fo great trefures as haue bin tranfported out of the

P

Indies into Spaine (the like quantitie of golde and siluer, neyther K. Salomõ, neither any other worldly prince euer had, sawe,
or heard of) there is none left, besids ý of that that was here before the Indies were discouered, there is nowe none to be foũd,
no neuer a whit. Hereof it commeth that thinges are thrise dea-
rer then they were, the poore that haue want doe suffer great
miseries: and your maiestie can not dispatch matters of great importaunce.

SO long as Lares bare sway and ruled, that was ix. yeeres, there
was no more care of teaching or bringing the Indians to saluation, neither was there any more labour employed, or once
thought of, to that purpose, then if they had been trees, stones,
dogges, or cats. He wasted great townes and fortresses, hee gaue
to one Spaniard 100. Indians, to another fiftie, to another more
or lesse, as euery man was in liking or fauour, and as it pleased
him to graunt. He gaue children, & old men, women with child,
and in childbed, men of countenance and commons, the naturall
Lords of the towns and countreys, he parted them among those
to whom he wished most wealth and commoditie, vsing in his
letters of commaund this speech following: *To you such a man,
are giuen so many Indians with their Cacique, them to vse in
your mines and affayres.* So as all, great and small, young and
olde, that could stand on their feete, men, women with childe, or
in childbed, one or other, trauailed and wrought so long as they
had any breath in their bodies. He gaue leue to take away maried
men, and to make them drawe golde, ten, twentie, thirtie, fourty,
or eightie leagues, or farther. The women remayned in farme
houses and graunges, in great labours about gathering of great
heapes for the making of the bread that they doe eate, which is,
to heape together the earth whiche they doe digge, and rayse
foure handfull hie, and twelue foote square, that is a giaunts labour, namely to digge the hard earth, not with mattockes or sho-
uels, but with   In other places they spinne cotten, and
doe such other worke, as are most meete for gaine and rayfing of
                                                        coyne,

coyne, so that the man and wife should not see one another in 8.
or 10. monethes or a whole yere, And at their meeting they were
so worne with labour and hunger, that they had no minde of co-
habitation, whereby their generation ceased, & their poore children perished, because the mothers through hunger and trauaile
had no milke wherewith to nourish them : This was a cause
that in the Ile of Cuba, one of vs being there, there perished in
the space of three moneths for hunger 7000, children, some desperate women strangled and killed their owne children , others
finding them selues with childe, did eate certaine hearbes thereby to loose their fruit, so that the men died in the mines, the wo-
mé perished in the farme houses, their whole generatió in a short
space decayed, and all the countrey lay desolate. The saide gouernour, to the ende without release to keepe them in continuall labour, stil gaue them away, and yet besides their great labours
he suffered them rigorously, & very austerely to be misused. For
the Spaniardes that had them in commaund, appointed certaine
hangmen ouer them, some in the mines whom the termed Mi-
niero, other in the farmes, that were called Estanciero: vnnaturall and pitilesse persons that beate them with staues and cords,
boxing them, pricking them with needles, and still calling them
dogs: neither did they euer shewe any signe of humanitie or clemencie, but all their dealings did consist of extreame seueritie,
rigor, and bitternesse , so as in troth it might be thought great
crueltie so to entreat or gouerne the verie Moores, being the
cruellest of all others, for all the damage that they haue done to
the Christians : where the Indians are more treatable , curteous, gentle, and obedient, then any other nation in the worlde,
Farther, when because of these Estancieros and Minieros, together with such labours as they put them vnto, some of them fled
into the mountaines, as making full accoumpt to bee killed,
the Spaniardes chose certayne officers who they termed *Algua-
zil del Campo* , that shoulde pursue and hunt them out of the
mountaines.

The gouernour had also in the Spanish townes and fortes,
certayne of the moste honourable and principall persons

about

about him whome hee called Vifitors, vnto whome alſo beſides
their other ordinarie portions that he had giuen them, he gaue in
reſpect of their offices 100, Indians to ſerue them. Theſe in the
townes were the greateſt executioners, as being more cruel then
the reſt, before whom *Athuaziles del campo* brought all ſuche
as had bin taken in this chaſe. The accuſer, hee that had them in
commaund, was preſent, and accuſed them, ſaying: *This Indian
or thoſe Indians are dogs, & wil do no ſeruice, but do day'y run
to the mountaines, there to become loyterers & vagaboundes:*
And therfore required they might be puniſhed. Then the viſitor
with his own hands boûd the to a pale, & taking a pitched cord,
in the Gallies called an Eele, which is as it were an iron rod, gaue
them ſo many ſtripes, & bet them ſo cruelly, that the blood running downe diuers parts of their bodies, they were left for dead.
God is witneſſe of the cruelties committed among thoſe lambs:
I am perſwaded that of the thouſâd part I can not rehearſe one,
neither can any other tell it as it ought. The labour that they
were put vnto, was to drawe golde, whereto they had need haue
men of iron, For they muſt turne the mountaines 1000, times
vpſide downe, digging and hewing the rockes, and waſhing, and
clenſing the gold it ſelfe in the riuers, where they ſhall continually ſtand in the water vntill they bruſt, and rent their bodies e-
uê in pieces. Alſo whê the Mines peraduêture doe flow with water, then muſt they alſo beſides all other laboures, drawe it out
with their armes. To be briefe, the better to comprehend the labour that is emploid about gathering golde and ſiluer, it may
pleaſe your Maieſtie to conſider, that the heathen Emperours (except to death) neuer condemned the Martyres to greater tormentes, then to mining for mettall: ſometimes they were kept
a whole yeere at the mines: but afterward perceiuing howe manie periſhed there, they decreed that they mine for golde but
fiue moneths, which was fourtie dayes in melting, during which
time they tooke ſome reſt.

And what was their reſt ? They during thoſe fourtie dayes,
made heapes of that which they ſhoulde eate, that is, they dig-
ged the earth, and caſt it on heapes as is aforeſaide, which labour doeth exceede, dreſſing of vines, or tilling of the earth.

Through-

Throughout the yere they ne.ter knew holiday, neither might be suffered from labour little or much. Besides that during all this toyle, they neuer had sufficient food, no not of *Cacabi* whiche is the common countrie bread, and being made of rootes doth but smally nourish except there be some fish or flesh to eate withal. Moreouer, they gaue them of that countrie pepper, and *Aies*, which be rootes like vnto nauetes, rostèd or sodden. But some Spaniarde, peraduenture meaning to seeme liberall in their diet woulde weekely kill a hogge for 50, *Indians*, whereof the *Aliniero* would consume two quarters, and part the other two among the *Indians*, giuing daily to euery man as great a peece as the *Iacekins* doe giue of holy bread in their Churches. Some there were that through nigardlinesse wanting meate to giue them, woulde send them two or three dayes abroade into the fieldes and mountaines, to feed where they might satisfie themselues with such fruite as hang on the trees, and then vppon the force of that which they brought in their guttes, woulde force them to labour two or three dayes more without giuing thē any one morsell to eate. For the loue of God therefore, let your Maiestie thinke what substance or strength those bodies naturally so delicate and feeble, and nowe almost consumed and oppressed with these trauailes, could gather of this food: also how it were possible for those that liued so sorowfull, heauie and woeful a life, in such labour without food shoulde liue long. The gouernour commanded they shoulde bee paide their day wages and expences for any labour or seruice that they shoulde doe to the Spaniarde, and their wages was three blanckes euery two dayes, whiche in the yere amounted to halfe a *Casteiin*, that is worth 225 *Maruedies*: wherewith they might buye a Combe, a looking glasse, and a paire of blew or greene beades. Yea, many yeeres they had nothing at all paide them, but hunger and stripes did so abound, that the *Indians* regarded none of this, neither sought any more but euen once to get a good meales meat, or to die for all, as wishing to forsake so desperate a life. He depriued them of their libertie, suffering the Spaniards to keepe them in such bitter bondage and prison as no man that had seene it, would or coulde once thinke for : not leauing them any thing in this worlde free

P 3   to

to vſe at their pleaſures : yea, notwithſtanding the beaſtes haue
ſome time reſt, and bée ſuffered to feede abrode in the fieldes, yet
woulde not theſe Spaniards that we ſpeake of, graunt the Indians any time or leaſure ſo to doe : but the gouernour himſelfe
would force them to an obſolute, perpetuall, forced, & vnwilling
bondage. For they neuer had their freewil to do any thing at al of
themſelues, becauſe the Spaniards couetouſnes, crueltie and tyrannie, was ſtil forcing them to ſome labour, not as captiues, but as
beaſts, that are led bound to do whatſoeuer man will appoint. A-
gaine, if at any time they were ſuffered to depart to their houſes
to reſt them, then ſhould they there find neither wife, children,
nor food : as alſo although they had there found any meat, yet
ſhould they not haue had time to make it readie : ſo that there
was no remedie but death. Thus grew they into ſicknes through
long and grieuous trauailes, and that was ſone caught among thé
as being (as is aforeſaid) of a very delicate and tender côplection,
& much againſt their nature it was to be thus ſodenly, contrary
to their wont, & vnmerciſully put to ſuch labours, & to be beaté
with ſtaues, & ſpurned at, beſides the calling of thé at euery word
Villacos, & vpbraiding thé, that they counterſeated ſickneſſe like
loytering loſels, becauſe they would not lobour. When the Spaniards perceiued the ſicknes increaſe, ſo as there was no profit or
ſeruice to be looked for at their hands, then would they ſend thé
home to their houſes, giuing thé to ſpend in ſome 30.40. or 80.
leagues trauaile, ſome halfe doſen of Radiſh or _Refortes_, that is a
kinde of nauet roote, & a little _Cacabi_, wherewith the poore
men trauailed not far before they ſho:ld deſperately die, ſom went
2. or 3. leagues, ſome 10, or 20, ſo deſirous to get to their owne
home there to finiſh their helliſh life that they ſuffered, that they
euē fel down dead by the waies: ſo as, many times we haue foûd
ſom dead, others at deaths doore, others groning & pitifully to
their powers pronouncing this word, _hunger, hunger._ Then the
gouernour ſeeing that the Spaniard had in this wiſe ſlaine, half or
two 3. parts of theſe Indians, whô he had giuen them in commaund, he came a freſh to drawe new lottes, and make a newe
diſtribution of Indians : ſtill ſupplying the number of his firſte
gift, and this did hee almoſt euery yeere.

Pedrarias

Pedrarias entred into the firme land, as a woolfe that had long beene ftarued doth into a flocke of quiet and innocent fheepe & lambs; & as Gods wrath and fcourge, committing infinit flaughters, robberies, oppreffions & cruelties, together with thofe fpaniards whom he had leuied, and laid waft fo many townes and villages, which before had bin replenifhed with people, as it were ant hilles, as the like was neuer feene, heard of, or written by any that in our dayes haue delt in hiftories. Hee robbed his maieftie & fubiects wirh thofe whom he tooke with him, and the harme that he did amounted to aboue four, yea, fixe millions of gold: he laid aboue 40. leagues of land defart, namely from *Darien*, where he firft arriued vnto the prouince of *Nicaraga*, one of the fruitfulleft, richeft and beft inhabited lands in the world. From this curfed wretch fprang firft the peftilence of giuing the Indians in commaund, which afterward hath infected al thofe Indies where any Spaniards doe inhabite, and by whom all thefe nations are confumed: fo that from him and his commandes, haue proceeded the certaine wafte and defolation that your maieftie haue fufteined in thefe fo great lands and dominions fince the yeere 1504.

When we fhall fay that the Spaniards haue wafted your maiefties, and laid you defolate feuen kingdomes bigger then Spaine, you muft conceaue that we haue feene the wonderfully peopled, and now there is no body left, becaufe the Spaniards haue flaine all the naturall inhabitants by meanes aforefaid, and that of the townes & houfes there remaineth only the bare walles: euen as if Spaine were all difpeopled, and that all the people being dead, there remained only the walles of cities, townes and caftles.

Out of the 13. reafon.

YOur maieftie haue not out of al the Indies one maruedie of certaine perpetuall & fet rent, but the whole reuenewes are as leaues and ftraw gathered vpon the earth, which beeing once gathered vp do grow no more: Euen fo is all the rent that your maieftie hath in the Indies, vain & of as fmal cotinuáce as a blaft of wind, & ỹ proceedeth only of ỹ the fpaniards haue had ỹ Indi
ans in

in their power : and as they doe dayly flay and rost the inhabitants, so must it necessarilie ensue that your maiesties rights and rentes doe waste and diminishe.

The kingdome of Spaine is in great danger to bee lost, robbed, oppressed and made desolate by forraigne nations, namely by the Turks and Moores, because that God who is the most iust, true, and soueraigne king ouer all the worlde, is wrath for the great sinnes and offences that the Spaniardes haue committed throughout the Indies, by afflicting, oppressing, tyrannous dealings, robbing and slaying such and so many people without law or equititie, and for the wasting of such and so large landes in so short a space, whose inhabitants had reasonable soules, and were created and framed to the image and likenesse of the soueraigne trinitie, and beeing gods vassals, were bought with his most precious blood, who keepeth account, and forgetteth not one of them: but had chosen Spaine as his minister and instrument, to illuminate and bring them to his knowledge, and as it had bin for a worldly recompence, besides the eternal reward, had graunted her so great natural riches, and discouered for her such & so great fruitfull and pleasant landes, and with al such artificial treasure, together with so many incomparable mines of gold, siluer, stone, and precious pearle, with infinite other commodities, the like whereof were neuer seene ne heard of : all which notwithstanding, shee hath shewed herselfe so vnthankfull, in yeelding euill for so many benefites which shee had receiued, And God ordinarily vseth this rule in executing his iustice & punishment, that is, that he chastizeth sinne with the same, or with that which is quite contrarie to that wherwith the sinne is committed.

The destructions, griefes, violences, iniuries, cruelties, and murders done and committed against those people, are so greate, horrible, publike & euident, that the teares, lamétations & blood of so many innocent persons doe ascende to the high throne of heauen, & doe not returne before they haue sounded in ẙ very eares of God, from whence they after descend, and straying ouer the face of the earth doe ring in the eares of al forraigne nations, so horrible and inhumaine as may be: wherupon ensueth among
the

the hearers great offence, horror, abhomination, hatred and infamie toward the kinges and commons of Spaine, whereof in time to come may ensue great damage.

Out of the said Bishop and authours protestation.

THose losses and detrimentes that by these occasions the crowne of *Castile* and *Leon*, together with the rest of spain haue susteined, as also such other spoyles and slaughters as hereafter will bee committed throughout the whole Indies, both the blinde shall see, the deafe heare, the dumbe publishe, and the wise shall iudge. Further in as much as our life is short, I doe take God to witnesse with all the *Hierarchies* and thrones of Angels, all the saints of the heauenly court, and all the men in the worlde: yea, euen those that shall hereafter bee borne, of the certificate that here I doe exhibite: also of this the discharge of my conscience, namely that if his maiestie graunteth to the Spaniards the aforesaide diuelish and tyrannous partition, notwithstanding whatsoeuer lawes or statutes shall bee deuised, yet will the Indies in short space be laid desart and dispeopled, euen as the Ile of *Hispaniola* is at this present, which otherwise would bee most fruitfull and fertile : together with other the Iles & lands aboue 3000. leagues about, besides *Hispaniola* it self and other landes both farre and neere. And for those sinnes, as the holy scripture doth very well informe mee, God will horribly chastize, and peraduenture wholy subuert and root out all Spaine. Anno, 1542.

The Prologue of Bishop Bortholo-
mewe de las Casas or Casaus, to the most *mightie Lord and Prince of Spaine,* Don Philip our good Lorde.

MOst high and mightie Lorde, of late I was moued and by the kings most vigilant counsaile for the Indies, vpon their zeale and honour that they beare to our Lord God; as also hartie

Q

loyaltie

loyaltie, wherwith they be adorned for his maiesties seruice, forced in writing to set downe suche matter as to your person by mouth I haue heretofore reported: namely, what I thought touching the title and claime that the kings of *Castile* doe make to the soueraigne and vniuersall principalitie ouer the Indians: notwithstanding, some did arise, who missliking that I dealt and trauailed with his maiestie and your highnes, about the discomfitures and losses compassed and perfourmed against the people of those countries, and reported that in as much as I did so far detest and with such bitternesse and sharpnes did abhorre them: as also I will still doe, so long as I liue, I doe call in doubt, and somewhat deminish the said royall title and right.

In which deede, as a testimonie what I did think, and in truth according to God and his holy lawe doe still hold, I exhibited 30. propositions, deuoid of all other proofe then what eache of them in it selfe did conteine, the one of necessitie following the other, because I was driuen to send them to his maiestie vnder pretence of the great counsaile that then was holden.

Afterward proceeding and persisting in desire to serue god by refelling somemens slanders, who either for want of comprehending the truth, or els hauing some other purposes & contrarie meanings, do presume vnder a fained and counterfet kinde of seruice to the kings (who of theselues naturally are endued with courteous & simple mindes and hearts, iudging & measuring all other by themselues) to present vnto them, a poysoned, bitter, & peraduenture a mortall drinke which doth not only waste kingdomes & common wealthes, in procuring their carefull calamities & dolorous destruction: but also doe bring euen the kinges owne persons to the pit of manifest danger & irreparable detriments and losses. With which fraudulous counsails they doe infect so much as in the lieth, the good & godly affections of kings, and do subuert all the princes vertuous deuises & studies. Hereof did sometime that most mightie king *Artaxerxes* otherwise tearmed *Assuerus* complaine, as appeareth in the booke of *Hester*. I haue so indeuoured my selfe (most mightie Lord) that now I haue set in hand the proofe of the said 30. propositions & some more, comprehending the whole in this brief summarie, which

is

is taken out of a greater volume, wherein euery article is more perticulerly expounded : herein setting in sight only the 17. and 18.proposition, because the whole substance of this matter may be reduced to these two propositions as to the principles & ends.

The title hereof should in my opinion haue been: *A probatorie tretise of the soueraigne Empire, and vniuersal principalitie, which the kings of Castile haue ouer the Indies*: As presupposing that it is manifest & proued, in that the Apostolike sea hath graunted it, and that there needeth no other opening of the reasons whereupon the graunt of this empire consisteth.

I purpose in this treatise chiefly to discharge my conscience, vsing that meane which it seemeth that Gods prouidence hath appointed me. My great age(for I am aboue 50.)being the cause of my large knowledge and eye experience of the Indian affaires, also to giue notice of that which passed in these partes, as also what was to be done, euer referring my self to the like desire that the disorders that I haue there seen practised might be redressed. And the rather because those that hinder this redresse & are most hurtful to those lãds, are such as being deuoid of truth & iustice, do indeuour by counterfeating and mingling that which is false, & vntrue, and withall seeming to doe it for your maiesties seruice, especially colouring your right to this new worlde, are in trueth altogether withstanders of your seruice & weale, either spirituall or temporall(as euery true christian & wise man wil graunt) The other benefite that I hope to obteine and reape by this treatise, is, that I shall detect and vnfold those mens errours, who rashly dare affirme that the right and principalitie of the kinges of *Castile* ouer the Indians is, or shoulde consist of armes and great force, entring vpon them euen as *Nemrod* who was the first hunter and oppressour of mankinde did euer, and establishe his principalitie, as the holy scripture testifieth: either as great *Alexander* and the Romans, and all other notable and famous tyrants, doe lay the foundation of their Empires : also as the Turke doth nowe adaies inuade, trouble, and oppresse christendome : and yet haue not any of them once approched the spanish tyrannies.

How far those men that do pronounce such a sentence do euill

seruice

seruice, and offend the sincertie and loue of the king of *Castiles* iustice, is here very easie to be iudged.

Who for proofe of their matters doe commit error vpon error, and so doe heape together other things both absurd, wicked and vnworthie to bee once hearde from these men which bee taken either for Christians or for reasonable persons. For vsually such as stray from vertue and truth, in excusing one fault, or mainteining one errour, doe runne headlong into many. Others there are that do colour them with fairer & honester titles, who also deserue to be reiected, reproued, & laughed at as those that say, because we haue more wit, or that we border neerest vpon them, either for that the Indians are infected with suche and such vices, we may subdue them: with other like colours wherwith they bee so far from vpholding or confirming that which they weene to strengthen and fortifie, that finally they lay all in the dust. To the end therefore that his maiestie may bee certified of all aforesaid, and as a most Christian and iust prince, may discerne betweene the pure and corrupt: also betwene right & wronge, and withall that he may knowe who serueth him faithfully, and those that hange vppon him only to satisfie their owne affections: and for their priuate profit doe inuent and deuise new titles for his Indies, which be neither probable nor of any effect, & so do hope to come to do their duties before that I were able. Further for that offering this treatise to your highnes, his maiestie shall bee serued thereby, sith himselfe shall haue such lettes there as he goeth, I doe most humbly beseech your highnesse in his name to accept it: also to examine, discerne, and vnderstande it with such wisedome and clemencie as you holde of his maiestie, and as himselfe would doe, seeing it is so, that Gods prouidence hath appointed your highnesse to inherite, as we doe hope the same right in the empire & principalitie of thē: besides if it seeme necessary to be published in other places outof this realm I will, if your highnes so command me, put it in latin: & although it should not deserue to be dispersed either in latin or otherwise, yet were not the losse great, in that I caused it to be printed onlie to the end your highnesse might with more ease reade the same, whose glorious life and royall estate, the Lorde increase and prosper, Amen.

The

The summe of the disputation between
Fryer Battlemewe de las Casas or Casaus, and
Doctor Sepulueda.

DOctor Sepulueda the Emperors chronographer hauing information, & being perswaded by certayne of those Spaniardes, who were most guiltie in the slaughters and wastes committed among the Indian people, wrote a booke in Latine in forme of a Diologue very eloquently, and furnished with all floures, and precepts of Rhetoricke, as in deede the man is verie learned and excellent in the saide tongue, which booke consisted vpon two principall conclusions : The one, that the Spaniardes warres against the Indians, were as concerning the cause and equitie that moued the thereto, very iust: also that generally the like war may & ought to be cotinued, His other conclusion, that the Indians are bound to submitte them selues to the Spaniards gouernment, as the foolishe to the wise: if they will not yeelde, then that the Spaniards may (as he affirmeth) warre vpon them.

These are the two causes of the losse and destruction of so infinite numbers of people : also that aboue 2000. leagues of the maine lande, are by sundrie newe kindes of Spanish cruelties and inhumaine dealinges bin lefte desolate in the Ilands: namely by conquestes and commaundes as he nowe nameth those which were wont to be called Partitions.

The sayde Doctor Sepulueda coloureth his treatise, vnder the pretence of publishing the title which the kinges of Castile and Leon doe chalenge in the gouernment and vniuersall soueraigntie of this Indian world, so seeking to cloake that doctrine whiche he endeuoureth to disperse and scatter as well in these lands, as also throughout the kingdomes of the Indians, This booke he exhibited to the royall counsaile for the Indies, very earnestly and importunately lying vpon them for licence to print it, which they sundry times denied him in respect of the offence, dangers, & manifest detriment, that it seemed to bring to the common-

wealth.

wealth.

The Doctour seeing that heere hee coulde 'not publishe his booke, for that the counsaile of the Indies woulde not suffer it, he delte so farre with his friendes whiche followed the Emperours court, that they gotte him a patente, whereby his Maiestie directed him to the royall counsayle of Castile, who knewe nothing of the Indian affaires: vpon the comming of these letters the court and counsaile being at Aranda in Duero, the yeere 1547. Fryer Bartholomewe de las Casas or Casaus, Bishoppe of the royall towne of Chiapa, by happe arriued there, comming from the Indians, and hauing intelligence of Doctor Sepulueda his driftes and deuises, had notice also of the contentes of his wholebooke: but vnderstanding, the authours pernitious blindnes, as also the irrecouerable losses that might ensue vpon the printing of this booke, with might & maine withstood it, discouering & reuealing the poyson wherewith it abounded, and whereto it pretended.

The Lordes of the royall counsell of Castile, as wise and iust iudges, determined therefore to sende the sayde booke to the Vniuersities of Salamanca & Alcala, the matter being for he most part therein Theologicaliy handled, with commaundement to examine it, and if it might be printed, to signe it: which Vniuersities after many exact and diligent disputations, concluded, that it might not be printed, as contayning corrupt doctrine. The Doctour not so satisfied, but complayning of the Vniuersities aforesayde, determined, notwithstanding so many denialles and repulses at both the royall counsailes, to sende his treatise to his friends at Rome, to the ende there to print it, hauing first transformed it into a certayne Apologie written to the Bishop of Segouia, because the same Bishoppe hauing perused the treatie and booke aforesaide, had brotherly and charitablie as his friende by letters reprooued and counsayled him. The Emperor vnderstanding of the impression of the sayde booke and Apologie, did immediatly dispatche his letters patents, for the calling in and supression of the same, commaunding likewise to gather in agayne all copies thereof throughout Castile, for the said Doctour had published also in the Castilean language a certaine abstract of the saide booke, thereby to make it more common to àll the lande: and to the ende alſo that the commons, and ſuch as vnderſtood no latine, might haue ſome vſe thereof, as being a matter agreeable and toothſome to ſuche vs coueted great riches, and ſought wayes to clyme to other eſtates, then eyther themſelues, or their predeceſſors coulde euer attaine vnto without great coſt, labour, and cares, and oftentimes with the loſſe and deſtruction of diuers.

Which when the Biſhoppe of Chiapa vnderſtood e, hee determined alſo to write an apologie in the vulgar tongu e, againſt the ſaide doctors ſummarie, in defence of the Indies, therein impugning and vndermining his foundations, and anſwering all reaſons, or whatſoeuer the doctor coulde alleadge for him ſelfe, therin diſplaying & ſetting before the peoples face the dangers, inconueniences and harmes in the ſayde doctine contayned.

Thus as many thinges paſſed on both ſides, his Maieſtie in the yeere 1550 called to Valadolid, an aſſemblie of learned men, as well Diuines as Lawyers, who being ioyned with the Royall counſaile of the Indies ſhoulde argue, and among them conclude, whether it were lawfull without breach of Iuſtice, to leuie warres, commonly tearmed conqueſtes, againſt the inhabitantes of thoſe conntries, without any newe offence by them committed their infidelitie excepted.

Doctor Sepulueda was ſummoned to come and ſay what hee coulde, and being entred the counſayle chamber, did at the firſt ſeſſion vtter his whole minde. Then was the ſayde Biſhoppe likewiſe called, who for the ſpace of fiue dayes, continually did reade his Apologie: but being ſomewhat long, the Diuines and Lawyers there aſſembled, beſought the learned and reuerende father Dominicke Soto his Maieſties confeſſour, and a dominican Fryer, who was there preſent, to reduce it into a ſummarie and to make ſo many copies as there were Lordes, that is fourteene, to the ende they all hauing ſtudied vpon the matter, might afterwarde in the feare of God ſay their mindes.

The ſayde reuerend father and Maſter Soto, ſet downe in the ſaide ſummarie, the doctors reaſons, with the Biſhops anſweres to the ſame. Then had the doctour at his requeſt a copie deliuered him to aunſwere : out of whiche Summarie

Q4   he ke gathered twelue against him selfe, whereto hee made twelue answeres, against which answeres the Bishoppe framed twelue replies.

Doctor Sepulueda his prologue to the Lordes of the assemblie.

MOst worthie and noble Lordes, sith your Lordshippes and graces haue as iudges for the space of fiue or sixe dayes heard the Lorde Bishop of Chiapa read that booke, whereinto he hath many yeeres laboured to gather all the reasons that either himself, or others could inuét to proue the cóquest of the Indies to be vniust, as seeking first to subdue barbarous nations before we preach the Gospell vnto them, which haue been the vsuall course correspondent to the graunt made by Pope Alexander the sixt, which all kinges and nations haue hetherto taken & obserued: it is meet, and I doe so desire you, that I who take vpon mee to defende the graunt and authoritie of the Apostolike sea, together with the equitie and honour of our kinges and nation, may haue the like graunt, and that it may please you diligently to giue me audience, while briefly and manifestly I do answere his obiections and subtilties: so doe I hope in God, and the trueth which I take vpon me to defende, that I shall plainely set before your eyes, and shew you that al ẏ is spoken on the contrarie part before so noble and wise iudges, who are not any way to be suspected of preferring whatsoeuer may be alleaged before truth and equitie which are of such importance, doth consist only vpon friuelous and vayne reasons. I will therefore, cutting off my speech come to the purpose. For it is small honour or curtesie to vse tediousnes among suche persons, beeing occupied in waightie affaires, namely, in the gouernement of the common wealth.

The Bishoppe of Chiapa his prologue to the Lordes of the assemblie.

Most

MOst worthie and noble Lords, right reuerend and learned fathers, hitherto in what soeuer I haue read, or in writing exhibited in this so notable and honourable assemblie, I haue generally spoken against the aduersaries of the Indian enhabitants of our Indies that lie in the Occean sea, not naming any, although I knowe some, who openly doe seeke to write Treaties thereof, and frame their grounde vppon an excuse and defence of suche warres as were, are, and yet may be prosecuted against those people, which haue beene the occasions of so muche mischiefe, so manye ouerthrowes, losses, and subuersions of suche and so great kingdomes, together with manie townes and infinite numbers of soules. Also that they subduing of those nations by warres, before they haue by preaching hearde of the faith or name of Iesus Christe, is a matter conformable to our Christian lawe: also that such warres are iust and lawfull, whereof it seemeth that the reuerende and worthie Doctor Sepulueda hath howe opened and declared him selfe the principall vpholder and defendour, in that heeanswereth to those reasons, authorities, and objections, that bee to the contrary: which in detesting the saide warres; and to the ende to shewe that the same beeing by another name, called conquestes, are wicked and tyrannous, I haue drawen into this our Apologie whereof I haue read part vnto your excellencies and Lordeshippes.

And seeing hee hath sought to disclose him selfe, and feared not to bee taken for the authour of so execrable impietie, whiche doe redownde to the slaunder of the faith, the dishonour of the name of Christianitie, and the domage as well spirituall as temporall of the most parte of mankinde: I thought it verie meete, as it is, so openly to impugne it, and for cutting off of the poysoned cancker whiche hee seeketh to disperse abroade in these countreys, to the destruction and subuersion of the same, to set my selfe as an aduersarie and partie agaynst him.

Wherefore I beseech your noble Lordeshippes graces and fatherhoodes, to way this so waightie and daungerous matter, not as any peculiar cause, for I pretende no farther, but to de-

R   fende

fende it according as becommeth a Christian, but as apperterning to God his honour, the vniuersall Churche, and the estate as well temporall as spirituall of the kinges of Castile, who are to giue accoumpt of the losse of soules alreadie perished, and hereafter to perish, vnlesse the gate be shutte vp against this heauie course of warres, whiche Doctour Sepulueda endeuoureth to iustifie. Also that this honourable assemblie admitte no Sophistrie by him vsed to couer and cloake his hurtfull opinion, whereby hee sheweth a pretence to colour and defende the authoritie by him called Apostolike, and the Empire, whiche the kinges of Castile and Leon haue ouer these Iudians. For no Christian can lawefully and honestly confirme and defende the authoritie teamed Apostolike, eyther the soueraignetie of any Christian king by vniust warres, by filling hilles and valyes with innocent blood, either with the infamie and blaspheming of Christ and his faith:

But the Apostolike sea is rather by suche meanes defamed and looseth her authoritie, the true God is dishonoured, and the true title and right of a king is loste and perisheth, as euery wise and Christian man may easily gather by that which Doctor Sepulueda him selfe hath propounded.

This title and right is not founded vpon the entrie into those countries, and against those people to robbe, slay, and tyrannosly to rule ouer them, vnder pretence of preaching the faith, as those tyrats entred & haue done, who by an vniuersall massacre and slaughter, haue murdered such a multitude of Innocentes: But it consisteth of a peaceable, louing, and gentle preaching of the Gospell, and of an vnfaigned introduction and foundation of faith, and of Christes principalitie. Yea who so euer goeth about to giue our Kinges and Lordes any other title, whereby to obtayne the soueraigntie and principalitie ouer those Indians, is starke blind, offendeth God, is a traitour to his king, and an enemie to the Spanish nation, whom he abuseth and most pernitiously deceiueth, seeking to replenish hell with soules.

Least therefore any of your Lordshippes graces or fatherhoods

hoods should stay vpon these damnable humors, it were meede as becommeth most chistian & wise men, yea, and very expedient to put to silence so hurtful and abhominable an opinion. And although in our Apologie, wee may seeme to haue satisfied, and at large answered whatsoeuer may be brought in defence of the said Apologie, yet because the doctor hath once againe propounded his defences, by parting father Sotoes summarie into twelue obiections, reason willeth mee to replie and shew that his obiections are friuolous, and to no purpose.

Out of which replies, heere followeth the abstract of two that stand vs in steede.

THE report is vntrue that the Indians did yeerely sacrifice in newe Spaine 20000. persons: either one 100. or you But had that been so, wee could not now haue found there so much people: and therefore the Tyrants haue inuented it, thereby to excuse and iustifie their tyrannies: also to deteine so many of the Indians as escaped the oppression and desolation of the first vintage, in bondage and tyrannie. But we may more truely say, that the Spaniards during their aboade in the Indies, haue yeerely sacrificed to their so dearely beloued and reuerende Goddesse *Couetousnes* more people, then the Indians haue done in a 100. yeeres. This doe the heauens, the earth, the elements, and the starres both testifie and bewaile: the tyrants, yea, the very ministers of these mischiefes cannot denie it. For it is euident howe greatly these countries at our first entrie swarmed with people, as also how we haue nowe laide it waste, and dispeopled the same: wee might euen blushe for shame, that hauing giuen ouer all feare of God, wee will yet neuerthelesse seeke to colour and excuse these our so execrable demeanours: considering that only for getting wealth and riches, wee haue in 45, or 48. yeeres, wasted and consumed more land then all *Europe*, yea and part of *Asia*,

R 2   doe

doe in length and breadth conteine, robbing and vsurping vpon that with all crueltie, wrong, and tyranny, which wee haue seene well inhabited with humane people, among whome there haue been slaine and destroyed 20. millions of soules.

In the last and twelfth replie as followeth.

THE Spaniardes haue not entred into *India* for any desire to exalt Gods honour, or for zeale to christian religion, either to fauour, and procure the saluation of their neighbours, no neither for their princes seruice, whereof they doe so vainely bragge: but couetousnes hath brought them, and ambition hath allured them to the perpetuall dominion ouer the Indies, which they as tyrants and diuels, doe couet to bee parted among them : and to speake plainely and flatly, doe seeke no other but to expell and driue the kings of *Castile* out of all that worlde, and themselues seazing thereupon , by tyrannie to vsurpe and take vpon them all royall soueraigntie.

FINIS.

Imprinted at London at the three
Cranes in the Vintree by Thomas
Dawson, for William Broome.

1583